The Intensification of Surveillance

The Intensification of Surveillance

Crime, Terrorism and Warfare in the Information Age

Edited by
Kirstie Ball and Frank Webster

Pluto Press

LONDON • STERLING, VIRGINIA

First published 2003 by Pluto Press
345 Archway Road, London N6 5AA
and 22883 Quicksilver Drive,
Sterling, VA 20166–2012, USA

www.plutobooks.com

British Library Cataloguing in Publication Data
A catalogue record for this book is available from the British Library

ISBN 0 7453 1995 5 hardback
ISBN 0 7453 1994 7 paperback

Library of Congress Cataloging in Publication Data
Intensification of surveillance : crime, terrorism and warfare in the
information age / edited by Kirstie Ball and Frank Webster.— 1st ed.
        p. cm.
   ISBN 0–7453–1995–5 (cloth) — ISBN 0–7453–1994–7 (pbk.)
   1. Privacy, Right of. 2. Electronic surveillance—Social aspects. 3.
Social control. 4. War on Terrorism, 2001– I. Ball, Kirstie. II.
Webster, Frank.
   JC596 .I58 2003
   363.25'2—dc21

2003007463

10   9   8   7   6   5   4   3   2   1

Designed and produced for Pluto Press by
Chase Publishing Services, Fortescue, Sidmouth, England
Typeset from disk by Stanford DTP Services, Towcester, England
Printed and bound in the European Union by
Antony Rowe Ltd, Chippenham and Eastbourne, England

2/03

Contents

Acknowledgements

This book was produced following a conference entitled 'The intensification of surveillance: Implications for crime, terrorism and warfare' held at the University of Birmingham in March 2002. The editors would like to thank the Birmingham Business School and the University of Birmingham School of Social Science for funding and hosting the conference. They would also like to thank the conference participants for their comments.

1
The Intensification of Surveillance

Kirstie Ball and Frank Webster

Surveillance involves the observation, recording and categorization of information about people, processes and institutions. It calls for the collection of information, its storage, examination and – as a rule – its transmission. It is a distinguishing feature of modernity, though until the 1980s the centrality of surveillance to the making of our world had been underestimated in social analysis. Over the years surveillance has become increasingly systematic and embedded in everyday life, particularly as state (and, latterly, supra-state) agencies and corporations have strengthened and consolidated their positions. More and more we are surveilled in quite routine activities, as we make telephone calls, pay by debit card, walk into a store and into the path of security cameras, or enter a library through electronic turnstiles. It is important that this routine character of much surveillance is registered, since commentators so often focus exclusively on the dramatic manifestations of surveillance such as communications interceptions and spy satellites in pursuit of putative and deadly enemies.

In recent decades, aided by innovations in information and communications technologies (ICTs), surveillance has expanded and deepened its reach enormously. Indeed, it is now conducted at unprecedented intensive and extensive levels while it is vastly more organized and technology-based than hitherto. Surveillance is a matter of such routine that generally it escapes our notice – who, for instance, reflects much on the traces they leave on the supermarkets' checkout, and who worries about the tracking their credit card transactions allow? Most of the time we do not even bother to notice the surveillance made possible by the generation of what has been called transactional information (Burnham, 1983) – the records we create incidentally in everyday

1

activities such as using the telephone, logging on to the Internet, or signing a debit card bill. Furthermore, different sorts of surveillance are increasingly melded such that records collected for one purpose may be accessed and analysed for quite another: the golf club's membership list may be an attractive database for the insurance agent, address lists of subscribers to particular magazines may be especially revealing when combined with other information on consumer preferences. Such personal data are now routinely abstracted from individuals through economic transactions, and our interaction with communications networks, and the data are circulated, as data flows, between various databases via 'information superhighways'. Categorizations of these data according to lifestyle, shopping habits, viewing habits and travel preferences are made in what has been termed the 'phenetic fix' (Phillips & Curry, 2002; Lyon, 2002b), which then informs how the economic risk associated with these categories of people is managed. More generally, the globe is increasingly engulfed in media which report, expose and inflect issues from around the world, these surveillance activities having important yet paradoxical consequences on actions and our states of mind. Visibility has become a social, economic and political issue, and an indelible feature of advanced societies (Lyon, 2002b; Haggerty & Ericson, 2000).

It is this intensification of surveillance that is the subject of this book. We concentrate our attention on the aligned surveillance surrounding crime, terrorism and information warfare, not least because, as Thomas and Loader observe, 'the transforming capabilities of ICTs make it increasingly difficult to distinguish between warfare, terrorism and criminal activities' (2000, p. 3). There are vital differences between these realms, but developments have led to a decided blurring at the edges, which lends urgency to the analyses and discriminations our contributors provide here. Moreover, the compass of these ostensibly discrete areas, something that extends all the way from suspicion and prevention to pursuit and punishment, is so enormous that they compel attention. Surveillance of crime can involve anything from observation of rowdy behaviour in the street to searching bank accounts for traces of illicit financial movements; from checking the rectitude of credit card holders to tagging prisoners released from gaol; from monitoring the speeds of motor cars to tracking Internet usage of suspected paedophiles. Meanwhile the pursuit of terrorists may call for anything from assiduous examination of airline bookings, identification of hackers, to satellite monitoring of shipping thought to be ferrying weaponry. And information warfare calls for nothing less than continuous and all-seeing observation of real and putative enemies – where terrorists are major targets and where criminal activity readily becomes pertinent – using the most sophisticated technologies available.

A particular concern here, perhaps inevitably, is with the period since September 11, 2001. The destruction by terrorists of the Twin Towers in New York city has stimulated, and perhaps even more importantly, legitimated, the acceleration and expansion of surveillance trends. Moreover, it has helped promote especially acute disciplinary forms of surveillance and it has blurred still more already fuzzy boundaries between crime, terrorism and contemporary warfare. To be sure, crime and terrorism have long been of major interest to surveillance agencies, but today we are witnessing a step change whereby there is a massive increase in surveillance, an expansion of those deemed deserving of scrutiny, and an integration of this with warfare itself. In this light consider the Pentagon's Terrorism Information Awareness (TIA) project, announced late in 2002. TIA has been developed as a response to September 11 and the consequent American priority of targeting terrorist threats (Goldenberg, 2002), which are now regarded as the major concern of the advanced societies' military. The TIA initiative aims to sift every electronic trail left behind in the US by terrorist suspects. The presumption is that terrorists exhibit patterns of behaviour that can be identified by 'data mining' many diverse and apparently mundane activities which are subject to surveillance of one sort or another. Accordingly, records of airline tickets, rental payments, traffic violations, bank statements, e-mails, immigration control, credit card receipts, parking tickets, telephone calls, ATM usage and the rest will all be accessed – and these through time so patterns may be discerned and evaluated. Similarly, video camera records from key locations (airports, monuments, public buildings etc.) and film from closed-circuit television cameras at freeway tollbooths, will be examined using facial recognition techniques to pinpoint suspicious people.

At the heart of Terrorism Information Awareness is the conviction that, by searching a vast range of databases, it will be possible to identify terrorists, even before they can strike. TIA will draw together the results of already prodigious surveillance activities in hopes that defence agencies will prove capable of spotting enemies before they cause mayhem. The premise is that, if everything can be seen, all obstacles and threats might be extinguished, and stability thereby assured. As its Mission Statement (DARPA, 2002) inelegantly puts it, the project 'will imagine, develop, apply, integrate, demonstrate and transition information technologies, components and proto-type, closed-loop, information systems that will counter asymmetric threats by achieving total information awareness useful for pre-emption; national security warning; and national security decision making'.

And who, post-9/11, might there be to object to this? There are undeniably serious terrorist threats posed to citizens, and it is surely right that all measures possible are taken against those who would perpetrate such crimes. Our main concern here would not be to resist TIA outright, but rather to draw attention to the mammoth amount of surveillance that *already* takes place and which is the foundation on which TIA builds. Focusing on the ordinariness of closed circuit television cameras in so many spheres of society, the ubiquity of the telephone system, the inescapability of credit card institutions, we want to emphasize the ongoing intensification of surveillance in everyday life. There are major consequences of this, to which we shall draw attention later in this introduction and to which our contributors pay heed, but at this stage we want to insist on the need to appreciate the spread of what might be thought of as ordinary and everyday surveillance.

Nevertheless, it is worth observing that, if the scale and scope of Total Information Awareness is awesome, it is neither unprecedented nor is its motivating spirit new (Bamford, 2001). Indeed, we believe that TIA is driven by a conviction that is familiar. This has it that order will be assured if all is known. If only everything can be observed, then, goes the reasoning, everything may be controlled. In this view, if surveillance can be thorough enough, then disturbances – anything from terrorist outrages to economic crisis, from late night fracas to the break-up of families – can be anticipated and appropriate action taken to remove (or at least mitigate) them. We would go even further: the thinking behind TIA expresses what might be conceived of as a *compulsion to surveille*, which is endemic in the modern world, where order and control are the requisites of all else.

For instance, in the early 1980s an alliance of military high-ups, elder statesmen (notably former UK prime minister Edward Heath and one-time head of the World Bank, Ford Motors, and the Department of Defence Robert McNamara), entrepreneurs and technological innovators came together to create IRIS (International Reporting Information Systems). The aim of IRIS was to sift and sort, in real time, vast information flows gathered from across the globe on matters such as commodity prices, insurgency, political machinations, and investment trends (St Jorre, 1983). The ambition of IRIS was to provide corporate and government clients with timely information, which would be accurate, immediately accessible and customized. The premise was that, to maximize effect and appeal to those who would pay the subscriptions, it was necessary to know everything, from anywhere, at any time, that might impinge upon the interests of those footing the bill.

Much the same compulsion to surveille was also evident in H.G. Wells's advocacy during the 1930s of a 'World Brain'. The science fiction enthusiast conceived this as a 'new world organ for the collection, indexing, summarising and release of knowledge' (1938, p. 159). This 'mental clearing house', the World Brain, was to Wells something to be wholeheartedly welcomed since the 'creation ... of a complete planetary memory' (p. 60) promised order and prosperity, the twins of progress. One must observe the consonance here with both the TIA and IRIS projects: surveillance is the prerequisite of effective control, and the better the surveillance, the more adequate will be the control and command that delivers progress.[1]

From instances such as these it is not such a big step to the metaphor that is most commonly evoked when commentators think about surveillance – Jeremy Bentham's Panopticon. This was an early nineteenth-century architectural design, applicable to prisons, schools and factories especially, by which people could be inspected from central points, though the inspectors themselves might not be seen by those whom they watched, while the inspected could not easily communicate one with another. The design was deliberate in its ambition to have the subjects watched, the watchers capable of seeing everything always, and the watchers unaware when the watchers might not be watching. Michel Foucault, in his enormously influential study, *Discipline and Punish* (1979), took the Panopticon as a central motif of modernity itself, adding that self-monitoring accompanies panopticism, with the inspected continuously feeling that they are subject to surveillance. Moreover, to Foucault the Panopticon is more than a physical place, since it also entails new 'disciplines' of order such as carefully timetabled events for each day and scrutiny of the behaviour of the inspected over time. In the Foucauldian view, when surveillance is accompanied by technologies such as computerized tills and video cameras, then we have entered an era of the Panopticon without walls (Lyon, 1994). Hence the 'carceral texture' persists and deepens in a 'disciplinary' society, though the actual walls of the prison may have been removed. Contemporary surveillance becomes here a noticeably intense and intrusive form of discipline, which depends on observation, assessment and analysis as matters of routine (Whitaker, 1999).

It might be noted that recent Foucaultian accounts of the panopticon tend to resist the suggestion that panoptic techniques have become homogenized and centralized (though it is hard to avoid precisely this conclusion from reading *Discipline and Punish* itself) in the hands of, say, linked transactional corporations or integrated government agencies (e.g. Bogard, 1996). Gandy (1998), for instance, asserts that it would be a mistake to assume that surveillance in practice is as complete and totalizing as the panoptic ideal type would have us believe. For instance, it may be that educational institutions and retail corporations operate as huge panoptic machines in themselves, but these are both internally differentiated and externally hard to access by others, while the surveillers within education and the retail industry are themselves surveilled by many other panoptic-like organizations such as insurance companies and tax agencies. In this sense, today's surveillance may more accurately be seen as at once more pervasive and less centralized than might have been imagined by earlier proponents of panopticism.

Another critic, James Rule (1998, p. 68), reminds us that the Panopticon may offer 'little help' in understanding new forms of electronic surveillance if the issue is whether people are subject to *more* or *more severe* forms of control. It might be emphasized here that more intensive surveillance can readily accompany an easing of direct control since careful watching may allow successful pre-emptive actions or even improved self-control from those who are aware they are being watched (Boyne, 2000). Thus contemporary panopticism may be more a question of how rather disparate individuals, organizations, state bodies and the media relate to surveillance technologies and how these influence what data is collected, where this goes, and what happens in consequence. Thereby surveillance may be increasingly intense, yet lead to less overtly punitive controls than hitherto, while it may also be more differentiated, complex and textured than earlier proponents of the Panopticon feared (or hoped).

Moreover, in electronically mediated worlds, our identities are digitally authenticated by what Lyon (2001b) calls 'tokens of trust' (e.g. an ID number), which identify individuals in the absence of face-to-face interaction. In providing these mandatory tokens of trust, the corollaries are, first, that we collude in our own surveillance, second, in doing so, we contribute to the overall movement towards greater intensification of personal surveillance, and third, we erode privacy because our autonomy in disclosing personal data is decreased.

SURVEILLANCE STUDIES

Given the raft of issues and controversies that pervade the intensification of surveillance, it is no coincidence that, over the last ten years, the sub-field of Surveillance Studies has developed. This brings together scholars from a variety of backgrounds: urbanists, sociologists, computer scientists, political scientists, and even organization theorists contribute. One of its leading lights, David Lyon, surveys the scene following September 11 in Chapter 2 here. Lyon (2002b) observes that surveillance is crucial to the identification and sorting of people and things. He helpfully distinguishes two major categories of surveillance, namely categorical suspicion and categorical seduction. We propose a further two types: categorical care and categorical exposure.

Categorical Suspicion involves surveillance that is concerned with identification of threats to law and order – with malcontents, dissidents and, at the extreme, terrorists. It reaches from disaffected and troublesome young men to organized criminals, and it extends, when it enters the realms of 'information war', to close observation and assessment of enemies within and without, using an array of advanced technologies from communications intervention devices to satellite cameras. Categorical suspicion encompasses all the policing dimensions of surveillance, and few dispute its necessity, though many are concerned about its boundaries and intrusions into the civil liberties of citizens.

Categorical Seduction points especially to the range of modern marketing which endeavours to identify behaviour of customers that they might be more effectively persuaded to continue as consumers. Consumer society is distinguished by its means of persuasion – design, fashion, branding, promotion, display, celebrity, product placement … . Surveillance also plays a key role in the perpetuation of this system, since accurate information is a *sine qua non* of successful marketing. For instance, retailers have introduced 'loyalty cards' primarily to track the patterns of consumption (Where do they buy? What do they purchase? In what quantities and with what regularity?), in order that customers be more precisely targeted by advertisements, special offers, and similar enticing offers.

Categorical Care draws attention to the surveillance directed largely at health and welfare services (though undoubtedly this merges, in some cases, with categorical suspicion). For instance, the development of medical records may be a requisite of more appropriate and timely interventions, while the identification of 'at risk' groups in particular locations demands close monitoring of phenomena such as morbidity, income and housing circumstances. It is difficult to imagine an effective welfare service that does not amass extensive records on its clients and, indeed, health, education and pensions have been enormous stimulants to the growth of surveillance.

Categorical Exposure is signalled in the major development of media and its increasingly intrusive character in the present era. Most commonly witnessed with regard to coverage of 'celebrities' of one sort or another (and 'celebrity' is a fluid term, capable of including pretty well any public figure such as politicians and civil servants should circumstances allow), exposure is nowadays characteristic of the tabloid press especially (though the tabloidization of media means that it extends far beyond). It is intrusive and persistent, as a host of cases in recent years has demonstrated (Mathieson, 1997). Anyone targeted for such exposure is sure to have their friends and family closely scrutinized, their biographies closely examined for any signs of suspiciousness, and their day-to-day activities given the closest inspection. Bill Clinton's pursuit by the media, apparently more concerned with his sex life than his presidential responsibilities in the mid- to late 1990s, provides an especially vivid example of such exposure. The pursuit of Cherie Booth, the wife of the British prime minister, first by the *Daily Mail* and later by most of the media, late in 2002, provides another.

WHY INTENSIFY SURVEILLANCE?

Given that new surveillance-based practices emerge at regular intervals, various explanations for the spread of surveillance have been offered. None of them, it might be emphasized, give much due to particular events, however cataclysmic these might be. Accordingly, we ought to be suspicious of those who point to 9/11 as the springboard for a 'new' surveillance. Whilst we would argue that 9/11 precipitated an application of surveillance techniques the magnitude of which we have not hitherto witnessed, this is not our primary contention. Our central contention would be that 9/11 encouraged an alignment of actors, organizations, debates and viewpoints, from different policy and academic spheres, all of which featured surveillance as a germane issue. Accordingly, national security was constructed as relevant to public and private sector positions on CCTV and crime control, Internet security, and consumer monitoring, with privacy issues temporarily taking a back seat. Indeed, Dennis (1999) reports that 70 per cent of Britons are happy to let companies use their personal data, on the condition that they receive something back, such as a personal service or other benefits. The attack on the Twin Towers has accelerated surveillance, but its steady progress was well developed before then. Indeed, the more persuasive accounts of surveillance trace a lengthy history. It may be helpful to review some of these here.

From the Marxian camp has come the argument that surveillance emerges from the imperatives of class struggle. Harry

Braverman's (1974) classic text, *Labour and Monopoly Capital*, contended that corporate capitalism devised modern management to oversee and monitor the labour process so that it might be in a position to organize better and simplify what gets done at the workplace in ways advantageous to itself. The underlying premiss of management's systems of scrutiny of the labour process was that the workers were not to be trusted and that what was involved was a struggle to control the shop floor, which, in its own interests, management had to win. Braverman believed that Frederick Taylor articulated this creed in his classic book, *Scientific Management* (1964), and drew heavily on this text to support his case. Later commentators have argued, drawing on the Marxian tradition, that workplace surveillance has intensified and that management has extended its reach to consumers who are nowadays closely surveilled so they may be the more effectively persuaded, cajoled and directed by corporate capital (Webster & Robins, 1986). Throughout there is the prioritization of power and interest, which motivates the spread of surveillance that one group may better control others.

Though there is surely a good deal in the Marxian approach, major problems for it are, one, the adoption of a crude class model of society that appears blind to graduations of inequality and position, and, two, how to account for the considerably more direct forms of surveillance endured by non-market societies. This latter point conjures the image of former Soviet societies, as well as the present-day People's China, in which spies and surveillance were and are routine. In comparison, the surveillance regimes of the capitalist West appear positively benign. But evocation of non-market societies leads us to the perspective on surveillance that is now described as Orwellian, after George Orwell's dystopian novel *Nineteen Eighty-Four*. This approach warns of the omniscience of the modern state (and superstate), and the attendant risks it carries of totalitarianism. Intellectually, Orwellianism stands in the tradition of the neo-Machiavellian scholars such as Vilfredo Pareto and Gaetano Mosca, who concluded that power is the basis of all relationships and that those exercising power do so ruthlessly and calculatingly, and who held a poor opinion of their fellow men's capabilities and capacity for harmony and goodwill. Orwell did not share this cynicism, though his dystopian novel expresses it forcefully.

The great sociologist Max Weber had a distinct, if underelaborated, view of surveillance and its relation to modernity. He regarded surveillance as a necessary accompaniment to the increased rationalization of the world, something most manifest in the inexorable process of bureaucratization, which was accompanied by inescapable inequalities and, moreover, trapped people in an 'iron cage' of rules and procedures that destroyed initiative and individuality (Dandeker, 1990). The image is conjured here of the lowly bureaucrat who is but a cog in the wheel of hierarchical organizations that cold-heartedly maximize achievement of their targets, be they more production of ball-bearings or processing of welfare benefits.

These then are the great themes of social theory as regards surveillance: it stems from class relationships, the pursuit of power, or the spread of what Weber termed 'instrumental rationality'. There is, however, another explanation of surveillance, one that accounts for its spread in terms of it being essential to living the way that we do. From this point of view pretty well everything that we do entails an element of surveillance. To gain leverage we must observe closely in order to make effective decisions. Such surveillance is at once personal (we look around ourselves, as well as inside at our own biographies, to ascertain what it is that we will respond to) and involves the garnering of information from others' surveillance (for example, we look more or less interestedly at reports of family breakdowns studied by experts to understand better our own circumstances and how we might most appropriately act). In this way, surveillance is an essential ingredient of what has been called the 'reflexive self', one considerably more self-conscious and capable of creating itself than its predecessors (Giddens, 1991).

Moreover, surveillance is now a requisite of our participating in today's world, since it is surveillance that enables individual choices and a genuine sense of self-volition. For instance, telephone networks routinely track every call that is made as an essential element of their operations. But it is precisely this intricate and all-seeing surveillance of users of the phone network (every call is registered exactly, in terms of time, duration and contact) that allows users to enjoy the extraordinary freedoms that modern telephony bring (with mobile phones one can contact pretty well anyone, anytime, provided one switches on the mobile). Much the same case may be made for credit and debit cards: they simultaneously surveille and thereby intrude into the individual's private life and allow those with access remarkable advantages in terms of day-to-day actions (no need for cash, foreign currencies, and so on).

It is important to recognize this paradoxical character of surveillance: it intrudes and enables at one and the same time. There is a similar ambivalence about surveillance when it is seen from the perspective of social inclusion and exclusion. To be included as a citizen in our society one must submit to being surveilled (to provide an address to the authorities, to enter a tax return when required, to submit to the recording of one's health details …), but in return one gets access to a range of desirable services (the vote, welfare rights, medical benefits …). Against this, one might endeavour to escape surveillance, but this is to invite both hardship and the attention of disciplinary agencies. Indeed, to be excluded in today's world means, at least for the majority, that surveillance will be directed at them as 'outsiders', as probable 'deviants', 'threats' or, more kindly, 'in need of help'. Bluntly, to be included one must submit to surveillance, while the excluded will be watched willy-nilly.

There are many well-rehearsed objections to the growth of surveillance. Prominent amongst these is a perceived threat to civil liberties. Many commentators are understandably concerned that information may be accumulated for nebulous ends, or by the wrong people, or that files will remain active when they are long outdated. There is a substantial literature, and associated social movements as well as legislation, concerned with the civil liberties aspects of surveillance (e.g. Campbell and Connor, 1986; Davies, 1996), and several of our contributors to this book raise similar fears and suggest safeguards. This is entirely proper since the surge of surveillance in recent years poses sharper threats to liberty than before.

There is also a well-established tradition of thought, in both the United States and Britain, that objects to surveillance on grounds of intrusions on privacy (e.g. Rosen, 2000; Garfinkel, 2000; Thompson, 1980). The issue of privacy always – and rightly – looms large in consideration of surveillance. Fischer-Hubner (2001), drawing on Westin (1967), helpfully distinguishes three main areas of privacy – territorial, personal (of the body) and informational (of information about oneself). In Europe, privacy rights have been enshrined in the Human Rights Act (1998), the detail of which has been left to member states to implement. A good deal of the debate surrounding the right to informational privacy employs arguments concerning relative amount of cost and benefit of the disclosure of personal information, and the point at which one's right to privacy ends (Moore, 2000). The argument proceeds thus: if technology is applied to find information for a worthwhile end that outweighs the costs to privacy, then the use of the technology for this purpose might be permitted (Friedman, 2000). This can be a deeply problematic judgement.

Tunick (2000) raises the question whether expectations of privacy are reasonable in the face of the new technologies of surveillance that appear in our everyday lives. He suggests that privacy can be violated if our right to disclose autonomously information about ourselves is removed. The same applies to a personal e-mail and a personal diary if both were read without authorization. So Tunick argues that our expectation of privacy hinges upon whether exposure can occur by 'mischance'. Privacy is thus violated when somebody happens to be passing, and takes the opportunity to snoop. This principle is as much applicable in the electronic, as it is in the physical realm, by the viewing of individual records, as opposed to an aggregated whole.

From what we have already argued in this introduction, it will be clear that a position of opposition to surveillance *tout court* is, in our view, infeasible. The fact is that some degree of surveillance is a requirement of contemporary ways of life. In consequence, the key issues revolve around the character and motivation of the surveillance (what categories of surveillance are being mobilized, and to what end?) and the point at which proper boundaries are to be drawn. These are questions properly asked and addressed by citizens as well as by politicians and lawyers.

What we would like to contribute to the discussion concerns the matter of identity and the difficulties and dangers surveillance raises for the self. We would do so by drawing on the insights of social psychology. First, we would note that the construction of files on persons does not mean that one 'knows' them in any conventional sense. It does mean that we have data recorded on them – about their buying preferences, about their physical location at a particular time of day, about their library book issues, their train journeys and so forth. But this is to track someone's actions, not to get inside their motivations and mentalities. As such, it is at best an approximation to who they really are. Further, the recorded data is but a snapshot in time, easily taken out of context, and devoid of the essential meanings with which humans accord their behaviours. Faced with an expansion of surveillance, it is as well to remember that it does not straightforwardly give access to the inner workings of the mind.

Second, surveillance does strive to illuminate the observed, to shine a bright light on subjects whom it would make transparent. In addition, those who surveille are frequently not known to the subject. Indeed, the surveillance can be a secondary product of a particular action, which sets the surveiller still further apart from the surveilled (for example, the payment of the meal may be recorded as a measure of a lifestyle pattern by the market researcher who melds it with other information, not simply as the transaction concerning the dinner imagined by the restaurant user (cf. Monmonier, 2002)). But this ambition and this secondary and unstated purpose are affronts to the self, both because there is something essential to one's identity that calls for limits on what may be known about oneself to others, and because to garner information for disguised purposes is morally dubious.

We would emphasize the importance to the self of there being limits to surveillance. The reason for this is that a transparent self is a non-self, one that can have no control over what is revealed to others, something surely essential to one's sense of being. To be sure, one does reveal oneself to one's intimate friends, but note that this takes place over time and in intimate circumstances, and typically involves reciprocity. That is, one reveals oneself to others by choice in terms of mutuality, trust and openness, in situations in which control is more or less equal. Surveillance takes away this control from the self, and endeavours to reveal its identity without discussion or reciprocity, thereby being an invasive force that strips the self of its independence and autonomy.

It is striking that tabloid media especially refuse to acknowledge or allow such differences. The justification of exposure of private matters (an affair, a financial arrangement, an old relationship) is that the public and the private should be at one, entirely consistent. Secrets have no place in such an outlook and are regarded as unconscionable by a media dedicated to exposure of hypocrisy, scandal and sleaze. But a moment's reflection surely reveals this to be a gross and potentially damaging simplification. Furthermore, without a delineation of borders between private and public (though it will not be a hard and fast line, it will be a real one), one risks driving away from public matters all but the most hardened and/or naive as well as assaulting the privacy of individuals (cf. Sennett, 1978). Who does not recognize the need for a private life, for the security of the opinion given in the intimacy of the home, for the difference between an off-the-cuff comment over a drink and one presented in an official setting? Erving Goffman (1959) probably overplayed the theatrical metaphors in his detailed explorations of the self, but his insistence that, to be human, we need 'backstages' where we can take refuge from 'performances' elsewhere, is telling. Secrets, in this sense, are an intrinsic part of being human – and, as with all secrets, the key issue is how and to whom they are to be revealed (Bok, 1984). This is not to posit that there is a realm of the public in which one deceives and distorts, while the private one is open and honest. It is rather to recognize that things are much more complex, context-dependent and layered than this. And it is also to stress that a search to have all revealed to the surveillance gaze is a threatening prospect for one's very soul.

Put like this, the stakes involved with surveillance can scarcely be higher. It is something that will not go away, and there is unambiguous evidence of an enormous extension of surveillance. In the post-9/11 context concerns about civil liberties and privacy have appeared to be of marginal significance, while the realms of crime, terrorism and information warfare risk becoming fused. The chapters in this volume are presented as ways of reaching a better understanding of contemporary surveillance so appropriate measures of resistance, and acceptable limits, may be put in place and secured.

NOTE

1. It is worth adding here that such examples undermine assertions that surveillance is a recent outcome of the application of sophisticated ICTs. While advanced technologies do facilitate and speed surveillance, the fact that Stalinist Russia and the entire Soviet regime were infected by secret police and spies is testimony to the efficacy of non-technological surveillance (Conquest, 1971).

2

Surveillance after September 11, 2001

David Lyon

The September 11, 2001 terrorist attacks on New York and Washington prompted a series of responses, from military retaliation on the country harbouring Osama bin Laden to extensive anti-terrorist legislation aimed at domestic protection. Among the latter, one of the most prominent ongoing reactions is to enhance surveillance operations on a number of fronts and there has been no lack of proposals concerning the best way to achieve this. Public money is being poured into policing and security services, and high-tech companies are falling over themselves to offer not just 'heartfelt condolences' for the attack victims but technical fixes to prevent such attacks from happening again.[1]

Sociologically, this raises many important and urgent questions. With surveillance, as in many other areas, it is frequently suggested that 'everything has changed', an idea that will stir the hairs on the back of any sociologist's neck. This sometimes reduces to a list of new gizmos on the everyday landscape, like iris scanners at airports, closed circuit television (CCTV) cameras on downtown streets and squares, and so on, or it can refer to a 'new era' of political control that overrides previous legal restrictions on monitoring citizens. (Curiously, in this context, commentators in Britain and the US have each warned against the 'police state' tactics of the other![2]) So, has everything changed, or not? I shall argue that the answer is yes and no. The underlying continuities in surveillance are at least as significant as the altered circumstances following September 11.

Focusing on the aftermath of September 11 is a worthwhile reminder that big events do make a difference in the social world. As Philip Abrams wisely said, an event 'is a portentous outcome; it is a transformation device between past and future; it has eventuated from the past and signifies for the future' (1982, p.191). To see events – and what I examine here, their aftermath – as sociologically important rescues our experiences in time from being merely moments in a meaningless flux. But the event is also, says Abrams, an 'indispensable prism through which social structure and process may be seen' (p. 192).

To take a notorious example, figures such as Hannah Arendt and, perhaps more sociologically, Zygmunt Bauman (1987), have helpfully viewed the Holocaust as revealing not merely the human capacity for evil but also some of the key traits of modernity itself. The triumph of meticulous rational organization is poignantly and perversely seen in the death camp, making this not just an inexplicable aberration from 'modern civilization' but one of its products. The reason that this example springs to mind in the present context is that today's forms and practices of surveillance, too, are products of modernity, and thus carry a similar ambivalence.

So what aspects of social structure and process may be seen through the prism of surveillance responses to September 11? I suggest that the prism helps to sharpen our focus on two matters in particular: one, the expansion of an already existing range of surveillance processes and practices that circumscribe and help to shape our social existence; two, the tendency to rely on techno-logical enhancements to surveillance systems (even when it is unclear that they work or that they address the problem they are established to answer). However, concentrating on these two items is intended only to mitigate claims that 'everything has changed' in the surveillance realm, not to suggest that nothing has changed. Indeed, I think it safe to suggest that the intensity and the centralization of surveillance in Western countries is increasing dramatically as a result of September 11.

The visible signs of putative changes in surveillance have both legal and technical aspects. The US and several other countries have passed legislation intended to tighten security, to give police and intelligence services greater powers, and to permit faster political responses to terrorist attacks (*New York Times*, 2001b). In order to make it easier to find (and to arrest) people suspected of terrorism, typically, some limitations on wire-taps have not only been lifted but also extended to the interception of e-mail and to Internet click stream monitoring. In Canada (where I write) the Communications Security Establishment may now gather intelligence on terrorist groups, probably using 'profiling' methods to track racial and national origins as well as travel movements and financial transactions. Several countries have proposed new national identification card systems, some involving biometric devices or programmable chips; others have brought forward more limited ID card systems, such as the new Canadian Immigration Card or the 'smart ID' for asylum seekers in the UK (*Toronto Star*, 2001; *Guardian*, 2001).

Some have questioned how new, while others have questioned how necessary, are the measures that have been fast-tracked through the legislative process. Sceptics point to the well-established UK–USA intelligence gathering agreement, for example, and to the massive message interception system once known as CARNIVORE, that already filtered millions of ordinary international e-mail, fax, and phone messages long before September 11. Debates have occurred over how long the legal measures will be in force – the US has a 'sunset clause' that phases out the anti-terrorist law after a period of five years – but few have denied the perceived need for at least some strengthened legal framework to deal with terrorist threats.

In some respects bound up with legal issues, and in others, independently, 'technical' responses to September 11 have also proliferated. High-tech companies, waiting in the wings for the opportunity to launch their products, saw September 11 providing just the platform they needed. Not surprisingly, almost all the 'experts' on whom the media called for comment were representatives of companies. Thus, for instance, Michael G. Cherkasky, president of a security firm, Kroll, suggested that 'every American could be given a "smart card" so, as they go into an airport or anywhere, we know exactly who they are' (*New York Times*, 2001a). Or in a celebrated case, Larry Ellison (n.d.), president of the Silicon Valley company Oracle, offered the US government free smart card software for a national ID system. What a commercial coup that would have been! He failed to explain, of course, what price would be charged for each access to the Oracle database, or the roll-out price tag on a national smart card identifier.

Other technical surveillance-related responses to September 11 include iris scans at airports – now installed at Schipol, Amsterdam, and being implemented elsewhere in Europe and

North America as well; CCTV cameras in public places, enhanced if possible with facial recognition capacities such as the Mandrake system in Newham, south London; and DNA databanks to store genetic information capable of identifying known terrorists. Although given their potential for negative social consequences[3] there is a lamentable lack of informed sociological comment on these far-reaching developments, where such analyses are available they suggest several things. One, these technologies may be tried but not tested. That is, it is not clear that they work with the kind of precision that is required and thus they may not achieve the ends intended. Two, they are likely to have unintended consequences, which include reinforcing forms of social division and exclusion within the countries where they are established.

A third and larger dimension of the technological aspect of surveillance practices is that seeking superior technologies appears as a primary goal. No matter that the original terrorism involved reliance on relatively aged technologies – jet aircraft of a type that have been around for 30 years, sharp knives, and so on – it is assumed that high-tech solutions are called for. Moreover, the kinds of technologies sought – iris scans, face recognition, smart cards, biometrics, DNA – rely heavily on the use of searchable databases, with the aim of anticipating, pre-empting and preventing acts of terrorism by isolating in advance potential perpetrators. I shall return to this in a moment, but here it is merely worth noting that Jacques Ellul's (1964) concept of *la technique*, a relentless cultural commitment to technological progress via ever-augmented means seems (despite his detractors) to be at least relevant.

So, what do these post-September 11 surveillance develop-ments mean, sociologically? Before that date, surveillance studies seemed to be moving away from more conventional concerns with a bureaucratic understanding of power relations (Dandeker, 1990) that in fact owes as much to George Orwell as to Max Weber. This puts a fairly high premium on seeing surveillance as a means to centralized power as exemplified in the fictional figure of Big Brother – the trope that still dominates many scholarly as well as popular treatments of the theme. Although some significant studies, especially those located in labour process arguments about workplace monitoring and supervision, see surveillance as a class weapon (Braverman, 1980), this view is often supplemented with a more Foucauldian one in which the Panopticon plays a part. Within the latter there are a variety of views, giving rise to a lively but sporadic debate (Boyne, 2000). One fault-line lies between those who focus on the 'unseen observer' in the Panopticon as an antetype of 'invisible' electronic forms of surveillance, but also of relatively unobtrusive CCTV systems, and those that focus more on the classificatory powers of the Panopticon (an idea that is worked out more fully in relation to Foucault's 'biopower').[4] The latter perspective has been explored empirically in several areas, including high-tech policing and commercial database marketing (Gandy, 1993; Ericson & Haggerty, 1997). Either way, data-subjects are seen in this Foucauldian perspective to be 'normalized' by surveillance, which is still thought of by many as an identifiable system of power.

While both aspects of the Panopticon offer some illuminating insights into contemporary surveillance, the latter has particular resonance in the present circumstances. In this view, persons and groups are constantly risk profiled – which in the commercial sphere rates their social contributions and sorts them into consumer categories, and in policing and intelligence systems rates their relative social dangerousness. Responses to September 11 have increased possibilities for 'racial' profiling along 'Arab' lines in particular, the consequences of which are already seen in the American detention of several thousand 'suspects' and a FBI trawl of more than 200 campuses to collect information about 'Middle Eastern' students (Steinberg, 2001).

Both the Weberian-Orwellian and the Foucaldian perspectives depend on a fairly centralized understanding of surveillance. However, given the technological capacities for dispersal and decentralization, not to mention globalization, some more recent studies have suggested that a different model is called for. The work of Gilles Deleuze and Felix Guattari (1987) offers some novel directions, suggesting that the growth of surveillance systems is rhizomic; more like a creeping plant than a central tree trunk with spreading branches. This has persuaded some to see surveillance as a looser, more malleable and flowing set of processes – a 'surveillant assemblage' – rather than as a centrally controlled and coordinated system (Haggerty & Ericson, 2000).

In the assemblage, surveillance works by abstracting bodies from places, splitting them into flows to be reassembled as virtual data-doubles, calling into question once again hierarchies and centralized power. One important aspect of this is that the flows of personal and group data percolate through systems that once were much less porous; much more discrete and watertight. Thus, following September 11, surveillance data from a myriad of sources – supermarkets, motels, traffic control points, credit card transaction records and so on – were used to trace the activities of the terrorists in the days and hours before their attacks. The use of searchable databases makes it possible to use commercial records previously unavailable to police and intelligence services and thus draws on all manner of apparently 'innocent' traces.

This brief survey[5] of surveillance studies shows how the once-dominant model of centralized state informational power has been challenged by socio-technical developments. The result is newer models that incorporate the growth of information and communication technologies in personal and population data processing, and more networked modes of social organization with their concomitant flexibility and departmental openness. But it is a mistake to simply leave the other kinds of explanation behind, as we move up (to the next plateau?) using something like Wittgenstein's ladder. To illustrate this, I shall simply offer a series of questions that once again allow the prism of September 11 aftermath to point up aspects of structure and process that relate in particular to surveillance.

Is surveillance best thought of as centralized power or dispersed assemblage? The responses to September 11 are a stark reminder that for all its changing shape since World War II the nation state is still a formidable force, especially when the apparently rhizomic shoots can still be exploited for very specific purposes to tap into the data they carry. Though the Big Brother trope did not in its original incarnation refer to anything outside the nation state (such as commercial or Internet surveillance that is prevalent today) or guess at the extent to which the 'telescreen' would be massively enhanced by developments first in micro-electronics and then in communications and searchable databases, it would be naive to imagine that Big Brother-type threats are somehow a thing of the past. Draconian measures are appearing worldwide as country after country instates laws and practices purportedly to counter terrorism. Panic responses perhaps, but they are likely to have long-term and possibly irreversible consequences. The surveillant assemblage can be co-opted for conventional purposes. With regard to the experience of surveillance it is worth asking, is intrusion or exclusion the key motif? In societies that have undergone processes of steady privatization it is not surprising that surveillance is often viewed in individualistic terms as a potential threat to privacy, an intrusion on an intimate life, an invasion of the sacrosanct home, or as jeopardizing anonymity. While all these are understandable responses (and ones that invite their own theoretical and practical responses), none really touches one of the key aspects of contemporary surveillance: 'social sorting' (see Lyon, 2002a). It is hard to get an adequate theoretical handle on this, and it does not help that no compelling metaphor – such as 'Big Brother' – has yet been proposed to give it popular cachet.

Yet the increasingly automated discriminatory mechanisms for risk profiling and social categorizing represent a key means of reproducing and reinforcing social, economic and cultural divisions in informational societies. They tend to be highly unaccountable – especially in contexts such as CCTV surveillance (Norris & Armstrong, 1999) – which is why the common promotional refrain, 'if you have nothing to hide, you have nothing to fear' is vacuous. Categorical suspicion[6] has consequences for anyone, 'innocent' or 'guilty', caught in its gaze, a fact that has poignant implications for the new anti-terror measures enacted after September 11.

The experience of surveillance also raises the question, how far do subjects collude with, negotiate, or resist practices that capture and process their personal data? Surveillance is not merely a matter of the gaze of the powerful, any more than it is technologically determined. Data-subjects interact with surveillance systems. As Foucault says, we are 'bearers of our own surveillance' but it must be stressed that this is not merely an unconscious process in which we are dupes. Because surveillance is always ambiguous – there are genuine benefits and plausible rationales as well as palpable disadvantages – the degree of collaboration with surveillance depends on a range of circumstances and attitudes. In the aftermath of September 11, it appears that anxious publics are willing to put up with many more intrusions, interceptions, delays and questions than was the case before, and this process is amplified by media polarizations of the 'choice' between 'liberty' and 'security'.[7] The consequences of this complacency could be far-reaching.

I have mentioned technological aspects of surveillance several times, which points up the question, are these developments technologically or socially driven? To read some accounts – both positive *and* negative – one would imagine that 'technology' really has the last word in determining surveillance capacities. But this is in fact a fine site in which to observe the co-construction of the technical and the social (Lyon, 2002b). For example, though very powerful searchable databases are in use, and those in intelligence and policing services are being upgraded after September 11, the all-important categories with which they are coded (Lessig, 1999) are produced by much more mundane processes. Database marketers in the US use crude behavioural categories to describe neighbourhoods, such as 'pools and patios' or 'bohemian mix', and CCTV operators in the UK target disproportionately the 'young, black, male' group. The high-tech glitz seems to eclipse by its dazzle those social factors that are constitutionally imbricated with the technical.

Still on the technical, however, a final question would be, are the new anti-terrorist measures pre-emptive or investigative? Over the past few years an important debate has centred on the apparent switch in time from past-oriented to future-oriented surveillance. Gary T. Marx (1988) predicted that surveillance would become more pre-emptive and in many respects he has been vindicated. This idea has been picked up in a more Baudrillardian vein by William Bogard (1996) who argues that surveillance is increasingly simulated, such that seeing-in-advance is its goal. A glance at any promotional platform of high-tech surveillance devices confirms that prevention of future occurrences is the supposedly clinching claim. However, this kind of argument easily loses sight of actual data-subjects – persons – whose daily life chances and choices are affected in reality by surveillance (Graham, 1998) as well as resting on dubious and seldom independent empirical tests.

Unfortunately, the attraction of new technologies that will be able to prevent future terrorist acts is strong in policy circles. It would be nice to believe in this anticipatory and preventive capacity – and as one who was in mid-flight over North America at the time of the attacks I would love to think it true! – but the overwhelming evidence points in the other direction. Surveillance can only anticipate up to a point, and in some very limited circumstances. Searchable databases and international communications interception were fully operational on September 10 to no avail. The likely result will be that internal surveillance of citizens by the state will increase. And if terrorists are apprehended it will be by other means.

Surveillance responses to September 11 are indeed a prism through which aspects of social structure and process may be observed. The prism helps to make visible the already existing vast range of surveillance practices and processes that touch everyday life in so-called informational societies. And it helps to check various easily made assumptions about surveillance – that it is more dispersed than centralized, that it is more intrusive than exclusionary, that data-subjects are dupes of the system, that it is technologically driven, that it contributes more to prevention than to investigation after the fact.

Sociologically, caution seems to be called for in seeing older, modernist models simply as superseded by newer, postmodern ones. For all its apparent weaknesses in a globalizing world, the nation state is capable of quickly tightening its grip on internal control, using means that include the very items of commercial surveillance – phone calls, supermarket visits, and Internet surfing – that appear 'soft' and scarcely worthy of inclusion as 'surveillance'. And for all the doubts cast on the risk-prone informational, communications, and transport environment, faith in the promise of technology seems undented by the 'failures' of September 11. Lastly, in the current climate it is hard to see how calls for democratic accountability and ethical scrutiny of surveillance systems will be heard as anything but liberal whining. The sociology of surveillance discussed above sees this as a serious mistake, with ramifications we may all live to regret.

NOTES

1. This may be seen on many Web sites, e.g. http://www.viisage.com
2. A leading article in the *Independent* (UK) warns 'Think again, Mr Blunkett, before eroding our most fundamental rights' November 12, 2001

http://argument.independent.co.uk/leading_articles/story.jsp while Jeffrey Rosen warns about the British surveillance situation as a road that should not be followed in the US. *New York Times Magazine*, October 2001.

3. See e.g. the debate over iris scans at airports, prompted by the American Civil Liberties Union (ACLU) but extending much more broadly as well. http://www.aclu.org/features/f110101a.html http://www.siliconvalley.com/docs/hottopics/attack/image101801.htm http://sg.news.yahoo.com/011102/12/lne83.html

4. Part of the difficulty is that although the idea of biopower exists in *Discipline and Punish*, it is much more clearly evident in *The History of Sexuality*.

5. A longer survey appears in David Lyon (2001a).

6. This elegant concept was first used by Gary T. Marx (1988). I discuss its commercial equivalent, 'categorical seduction' in Lyon (1994).

7. I experienced this, anecdotally, when an op-ed piece I wrote under the title 'Whither surveillance after bloody Tuesday?' was published in the newspaper as 'What price in liberty will we pay for security?' The *Kingston Whig-Standard*, September 28, 2001.

3
Data Mining and Surveillance in the Post-9/11 Environment

Oscar H. Gandy

In his wildly successful book on the future of cyberspace Lawrence Lessig (1999) responded to a general challenge to privacy activists: tell us what is different about surveillance in the computer age. Lessig suggested that the difference is to be seen in the ease with which the data generated from the routine monitoring of our behaviour can be stored, and then searched at some point in the future.

Indeed, because more and more of our daily life involves interactions and transactions that generate electronic records, our lives become fixed in media that can be examined and reviewed at will. Lessig and others who are concerned about threats to privacy (Lyon, 2001a) have identified the countless ways in which our behaviour in public places, as well as in the privacy of our homes, generates records that come to reside in the computers of corporations and government agencies.

As Lessig suggests, while a sales clerk in the local store might take note of a shopper's interest in different pieces of jewellery or clothing as she makes her way from counter to counter, their monitoring does not generate a searchable record of each of her visits to the store. Indeed, unless they are security guards, and she is looking particularly suspicious that day, the guards usually don't follow her from floor to floor. It is only when she actually purchases those socks or gloves that a searchable record is made. However, the generation of searchable records of 'transactions' in electronic network environments (cyberspace) is many times more extensive than it is in the world of bricks and mortar. Web servers generate a record each time a visitor clicks on a banner ad, or follows a link in order to learn more about some commodity or service.

In addition, because of the ways in which Web technology facilitates the linkage of records, the click streams, or mouse droppings that surfers leave behind as they browse around much of the Web, makes it easy for marketing service providers like DoubleClick to develop a cumulative record (Sovern, 1999). Because DoubleClick manages the serving of ads for several thousand publishers on the Web, individual profiles may contain information about a broad range of goods and services about which an individual may have indicated some interest.

Because the cost of storing data in electronic form continues to drop (one theoretical estimate, based on what engineers refer to as Moore's law, suggests that the cost of storage drops by 50 per cent every 18 months), there is less of an incentive for organizations to discard any transaction-generated information (Gates, 1999). The problem that businesses and government agencies are then left with is determining how to make sense of these growing mountains of data (Green et al., 1999).

Enter the mathematical wizards who brought us both the bell curve and the ballistic missile, and *voilà*! we have the science of data mining, or as the specialists would prefer, the science of Knowledge Discovery in Databases.

Data mining, as a tool for the discovery of meaningful patterns in data, is the product of some rapidly developing techniques in the field of applied statistical analysis. Of particular importance for those of us who are concerned about the implications of data mining for individual and collective privacy, is the fact that data mining software, products, and services are being introduced into the market place by a large number of competing vendors. The increasing sophistication of these software packages, and the rapidly declining prices for custom, as well as off-the-shelf data mining products means that these techniques will soon be in widespread use (Danna & Gandy, 2002).

In addition, governments' heightened concern with security following the events of September 11, 2001 (9/11) means that an infusion of tax dollars for research and development is likely to attract a swarm of competitors. We can expect this increase in demand to support an even more rapid development of the capacity of data mining programs to produce strategic 'intelligence' from what would ordinarily be meaningless bits of data stored in remote computers around the globe. The consequences of such a development are quite troubling, and they are the focus of this chapter.

What I will attempt to do in this chapter is provide a thumbnail sketch of data mining as a technology, identify some of the leading firms and the nature of their data mining products, and then identify some of the concerns that have arisen among privacy advocates, and others who are concerned about democracy and the public sphere.

DATA MINING

As I have suggested, data mining is an applied statistical technique. The goal of any data mining exercise is the extraction of meaningful intelligence, or knowledge, from the patterns that emerge within a database after it has been cleaned, sorted and processed. The routines that are part of a data mining effort are in some ways similar to the methods that are used to extract precious minerals from the soil. However, whereas the extraction of precious metals is often labour intensive, and represents risks to both workers and the environment, the extraction of intelligence from computer databases is increasingly automated in ways that reduce the direct risks to labour at the same time that they amplify the risks to society in general. Indeed, as I will argue, the impact of data mining on the social environment may, in the long run, be more destructive than strip mining for coal.

Imagine if you can, the mountains of transactional data that are generated each time a consumer purchases commodities that have been marked with universal product codes (UPCs). When consumers use credit or cheque verification cards, or any of a number of retail vendors' discount cards, individually identifiable information is captured and linked with the details of those purchases. There is little wonder that large retail chains like Wal-Mart have been forced to invest substantial resources in the development of data warehouses to allow them to extract some of the hidden value in the terabits of data being generated each day throughout their expanding global networks (Gates, 1999, p. 232).

Our interactions with government agencies, as well as with the component parts of the massive health care system, also generate detailed records. However, because these data are not gathered in standard forms with classification schemes akin to the UPC code, there are tremendous pressures within these industries to move toward greater standardization and comparability across transactions (Bowker & Star, 1999).

Although progress is being made somewhat more slowly in translating voice messages into text for automated processing, no such barriers exist for classifying e-mail text or the posts that are made to newsgroups. The textual components of Web pages are also relatively easy to classify and describe, although the graphics on those pages still represent something of a problem for developers.

Even more problematic, in terms of the need to develop common codes and classification standards, is the digitized output of surveillance cameras. However, it seems likely that the rate of success in developing classification techniques in this arena will increase substantially in response to research and development initiatives rushed through the legislature in response to the events of 9/11.

THE GOALS OF DATA MINING

In general, data mining efforts are directed toward the generation of rules for the classification of objects. These objects might be people who are assigned to particular classes or categories, such as 'that group of folks who tend to make impulse buys from those displays near the checkout counters at the supermarket'.

The generation of rules may also be focused on discriminating, or distinguishing between two related, but meaningfully distinct classes, such as 'those folks who nearly always use coupons', and 'those who tend to pay full price'.

Among the most common forms of analysis are those that seek to discover the associative rules that further differentiate between clients or customers. For example, video rental stores seem to be interested in discovering what sorts of movies tend to be rented together, and what sorts of movies tend to be associated with the sale of microwave popcorn or candy.

In an attempt to develop reliable sorting tools, data miners seek to discover patterns of association between demographic characteristics and a host of commercial behaviours. Discriminant analyses within the commercial sphere are often applied to the task of differentiating between high-value and low-value customers. For example, in the case of urban retailers negotiating the placement of radio advertisements, this sort of analysis may help them to determine what sorts of ads are more likely to generate 'prospects, rather than suspects' (Ofori, 1999, sec. 2, p. 27). That is, advertisers make use of strategic assessments based on estimates of the racial composition of the audiences they purchase access to when buying broadcast time. These choices are based on the belief that African-American and Hispanic youth are more likely to steal than to purchase certain retail products.

Businesses seek to maximize profits by minimizing risk. They do this by identifying individuals, who, by virtue of their profiles, ratings, or comparative scores, should probably be ignored, avoided or treated with the utmost deference and respect. Some business service providers may also rely upon the pattern recognition features of data mining programs to determine whether a credit card is likely to have been stolen, or if the legitimate owner of the card is at increased risk of default, or is likely to make a fraudulent claim.

Retail firms are increasingly likely to utilize risk avoidance programs in an attempt to identify patterns of behaviour that suggest elevated risk (Cavoukian, 1998). Starbucks reportedly makes use of a data mining package called RiskIntelligence to help it reduce its exposure to lawsuits based on in-store accidents. In order for risk minimization efforts to pay off for an organization like Starbucks, which has many hundreds of outlets, these sophisticated models have to incorporate representations of dozens of different floor plans and configurations. In addition, risk estimates have to include assessments of the distribution of accidents by time of day, and season of the year. Clearly, such incident data will have different interpretations depending upon the part of the country in which a store is located (Roberts-Witt, 2001).

Risk management takes on a slightly different character when the decision makers are involved in the protection of public safety or 'national security'. Data mining specialists at the MITRE Corporation described one project that involved developing a strategy for identifying or targeting vehicles for inspection by law enforcement officers (Rothleder, Harris & Bloedorn, (n.d.)). The challenges involved in selecting one vehicle from among many are presented as being similar to the problems involved in discovering patterns in aircraft accidents that would allow risk managers to identify the 'precursors' of dangerous situations in the air.

In the aviation example, an analysis of accident descriptions derived from on-board data recorders, or in the transcripts of witnesses, might reveal a meaningful pattern. For example, an analysis of accident reports might produce a suggestion that accidents often occurred following an indication in the records of air traffic controller commentary that the plane 'veered to the left following take-off'. Further analyses of accident records might indicate that such references were also more likely to be made when a particular class of malfunctions occurred under winter weather conditions. Each accident that is accompanied with a voice record provides data that can be transformed into text which can be searched for keywords, or terms that become more meaningful with each recorded accident. Over time, such terms become associated with a specific technical problem, while at the same time they can be distinguished from other terms or phrases that might indicate a mistake, or a pilot error. Ideally, the analysis of subsequent accidents adds to the power of the explanatory models that data mining helps to produce.

In the case of motor vehicle targeting, the focus of the data mining effort is slightly different. Here the effort is directed towards identifying the attributes of both the driver and the vehicle, as both are parts of the profile that is used to identify likely targets. In the case of airplane accidents, each one is examined in great detail. Not all automobiles are stopped, and all those stopped are not subject to detailed examination. However, each time a vehicle is subjected to a more detailed inspection, considerably more information is added to the pool of data about drivers and vehicles. Clearly the sorts of data that can be gathered during a full inspection, to say nothing of the data that might be gathered after an arrest, are substantially different from data that can be gathered on the basis of observation of a moving vehicle, or a cursory inspection of a vehicle when stopped.

Much has been written about the use of a driver's race as an element in the profiles used by state police to identify vehicles they believe are likely to be involved in the transportation of contraband drugs (Allen-Bell, 1997). Because of the adverse public response to the use of race as a predictor, data mining efforts are being turned toward finding other cues that the police may find to be equally useful, but less politically sensitive, indicators of a basis for justifying a non-random stop and search.

DATA MINING TECHNOLOGY

The technology of data mining becomes more sophisticated with each passing day. Neural networks are just one of the more sophisticated analytical resources being used more widely in data mining applications. Neural nets are said to mimic the ways in which the human brain processes information. These systems learn, or become more accurate, over time. An experience-based learning model attaches and adjusts the weights that are applied to different attributes or variables in response to each correct and incorrect prediction or determination.

A common application of neural networks by insurers is in support of fraud detection. In deciding whether a reported accident could have been staged, an analytical model is likely to have been developed on the basis of an assessment of detailed records from thousands of reported accidents. A relatively small proportion of these accident reports will have been determined to be fraudulent. At each iteration in the development cycle, varying weights will be assigned to potentially relevant factors such as the age and gender of the driver. As the model is developed, other, potentially more reliable, indicators may emerge. It will matter, for example, whether the injured party called an attorney. More importantly, perhaps, information about whether the claimant's physician was called before or after the attorney was called, might be added to the model. As usual, the desired outcome is an improved ability to make a prediction, and provide an estimate of its accuracy. The decision support system asks 'How likely is a particular item to be a fraudulent claim?' It is up to the client or user of the software to decide whether or not to just pay the claim, or risk angering the insured by requesting additional information about the accident.

Some applications systems allow their users to view case descriptions, navigate through the details, and then generate a variety of recommendations on a specific case derived from an analysis of multidimensional databases stored in remote locations. Although it is clear that the widely available systems have a long developmental path that has yet to be covered, it is not difficult to imagine a sophisticated user of an advanced decision support system in future pulling out her combination PDA/telephone, in order to choose which of a set of competing strategies she should use with a client she is about to meet for a working lunch.

While to some, that scenario may seem like science fiction, industry analysts suggest that in five years' time, e-business firms will have moved 'business intelligence' of this sort to the average desktop in the same way that Microsoft Word and Excel have become commonplace (Liautaud, 2001).

COMMERCIALLY AVAILABLE DATA MINING SOFTWARE

A number of firms have begun to offer data mining services and software products that are supposed to make it easier for Web-based marketers to transform transaction-generated data into intelligence that can be used to facilitate customer segmentation. Well-defined segmentation schemes often become the primary resource of a marketing campaign. Among the leaders of this emerging market are firms with names like digiMine, Accrue, NetGenesis and Personify. These firms provide analytical services to Web-based companies.

The emerging market also includes familiar providers of statistical software such as SPSS (Statistical Package for the Social Sciences), which includes neural networks and rule induction features in its Clementine Service resource. Some comprehensive software packages, or client service products, are designed to facilitate customer relationship management (CRM). Within marketing circles the philosophy of CRM is no longer one of capturing the largest share of the market; rather it is capturing the largest share of the most valuable customer's business (Peppers & Rogers, 1997). This is an orientation to the market that reflects a belief that 20 per cent of a firm's customers will provide 80 per cent of its revenue. Corporate strategists believe that capturing that revenue can be assured only by 'growing the customer' through 'cross-selling'. It also requires identifying those customers that are unlikely to grow, and then finding subtle ways to suggest that 'it's time for them to go', because 'they are the weakest link' in the relationship between the firm and its most profitable customers.

INCREASED DEMAND FOR DATA MINING TOOLS

While the firms that are providing the bulk of these data mining products and services will continue to try and shape consumer demand through aggressive marketing, they are also likely to realize something of a windfall in terms of the increased attention to the development and implementation of data mining applications following the events of 9/11.

Less than a week after the assault on the Pentagon and the World Trade Center towers, an article in the business section of *USA Today* asked, 'What can tech companies do?' Jump-start the development and implementation of data mining techniques, was the unequivocal response. One executive from one of a handful of still-active Internet communications firms suggested that '[we] are experts at data mining and we have vast resources of data to mine. We have used it to target advertising. We can probably use it to identify suspicious activity or potential terrorists' (Maney, 2001, p. 613). This executive was probably referring to applications such as 'Online Preference Marketing' (OPM), through which an Internet user's browsing activities are classified into 'types of inferred interests or behaviors that may be attractive to advertisers' (Agreement, 2002, p. 7). It seems likely that it was one or more 'volunteers' within the communications industry who provided the information that was used to identify some of the so-called 'material witnesses' in the United States detained by the FBI. The primary change, of course, would be the development of indicators and categories that would be of interest to government offices charged with insuring 'homeland security' in the US (*National Strategy*, 2002).

Much more cautious responses were offered by other technology developers who suggested that we were probably still years away from the kinds of data mining technology that might have allowed us to predict and interrupt the plans of the hijackers (Maney, 2001). Nevertheless, in response to what they perceived to be a continuing threat of terrorism, the Pentagon announced a major initiative designed to speed the development of technologies that could actually be deployed in the 'war against terrorism' within 12–18 months (Streitfeld & Piller, 2002).

At the top of the government's wish list was an appeal for 'ideas to identify and track down suspected terrorists, and to predict their future behavior'. This goal was linked with a desire to 'develop an integrated information base and a family of data mining tools and analysis aids'. What the Pentagon was looking for was an analytical resource that would assist in the 'identification of patterns, trends, and models of behavior of terrorist groups and individuals … . The system would allow "what if" type modeling of events and behavioral patterns and result in predictive analysis products.' Ideally, the Pentagon sought a system that could efficiently scan data in the nation's computer networks and if they 'discover that a member of an extremist group also bought explosives and visited a Web site about building demolition, they might be able to halt a potential attack' (France et al., 2001).

Commercial vendors were also invited to 'develop a deception detection device for use with counter-terrorism-based structured interviews for passengers of the various modes of transportation'. Essentially, the Pentagon was hoping to be able to acquire a reliable, portable and efficient polygraph device (Veale, 2001).

There are of course a great many reasons for being concerned about the sorts of dramatic changes in the ways in which the American government plans to escalate the surveillance of its citizens, their associates, and any visitors who might be defined as threats to the security of the 'homeland' under the broad powers granted under the USA PATRIOT Act (Bowman, 2002). These concerns are multiplied in the face of evidence that the United States government has been able to win compliance, if not active support, for its plans to increase the level of communications and data surveillance to be carried out on the citizens of other nations. Yet, there are, in my view, still more important concerns that are raised by visions of a tidal wave of commercial applications of data mining that will follow rapidly behind a Schumpeterian swarm of innovations (Preston, 2001) brought into being by this most recent activation of the military industrial complex.

The exchange of data mining applications between the government and commercial sectors is likely to be accelerated as a result of increased pressure and latitude for surveillance and data-sharing activities that have been approved under the extensive powers authorized by the USA PATRIOT Act (2001). There is particular concern about the availability of details about individuals' searching of the Web (Bowman, 2002), in that the capture of URLs from public terminals and private computers provides easy access to the content of files accessed by individual users (FBI asks ... , 2002; Government, Internet Industry, 2002; Madsen, 2001).

Federal agencies are expected to increase their use of techniques that have become quite common within industry. In the view of one industry observer,

> As the blindfolds are removed, today's FBI agents will quickly discover a world rich in information, from public chat rooms on the Web to commercially available databases that focus on financial records to other databases that provide details on dubious public figures around the world and their known associates. ... Perhaps one measure of success will be the day when among FBI agents there are more database experts than lawyers. (Crovitz, 2002)

SOCIAL IMPLICATIONS OF DATA MINING

Why should the expansion of data mining systems and applications concern us? As I have suggested, data mining systems are designed to facilitate the identification and classification of individuals into distinct groups or segments. From the perspective of the commercial firm, and perhaps for the industry as a whole, we can understand the use of data mining as a discriminatory technology in the rational pursuit of profits. However, as members of societies organized under more egalitarian principles, we have come to the conclusion that even relatively efficient techniques may be banned or limited to the degree that they are accompanied by negative social consequences, or externalities.

For example, Marsha Stepanek (2000) of *Business Week* referred to the application of data mining techniques in electronic commerce as 'Weblining'. I suspect she chose this term precisely because she believed that it would activate the collective distaste that Americans have expressed toward spatial, or geo-demographic, discrimination against neighbourhoods and communities defined by race. Indeed, these are techniques that the courts and legislatures have banned as 'redlining' when used by banks and mortgage firms.

However, because the Internet is only marginally defined by geography (Graham & Marvin, 2001), the 'neighbourhoods' that will be excluded from access to goods and services are primarily conceptual or analytical, rather than spatial. Because of this, the victims of 'Weblining' are less likely to be aware of their status as victims of categorical discrimination. As a result, they will be even less likely to organize as an aggrieved group in order to challenge their exclusion from opportunities in the market place, or in the public sphere.

Let me be clear. There are some people who argue that even the use of race, gender and age as elements within predictive models should be allowed because they are economically efficient (Hausman & McPherson, 1996). That is, because of the relatively high correlation between personal attributes like race, class and gender, and a host of other status and behavioural indicators, these data facilitate rational discrimination. In addition, because these indicators are relatively inexpensive to capture and interpret it would be inefficient and irrational to bar their use in decision-making.

On the other hand, those of us who argue against this sort of discrimination are concerned that if we allow decision makers to use race, and gender, and other markers of group identity as the basis for exclusion from opportunity, then we will only strengthen the correlation between group membership and social status.

African-American males provide the most obvious examples. The use of race as a bar to employment leads quite reasonably to a belief among African-Americans that investment in education makes little sense. The self-fulfilling prophesy takes shape and acquires material force through just this sort of iterative process.

Of course, it is not only discrimination on the basis of race, gender or age that should concern us. Our concerns should be based more generally on what we understand to be the social consequences that flow from using a decision system that systematically bars members of groups or segments of the population from acquiring the informational resources that are essential to their individual development and their collective participation in the economy and in the public sphere.

As a communications scholar, I am especially sensitive to the use of discriminatory technologies like data mining to determine which people will have access to the information that they need to make sense of the world. When data mining systems are used by companies in the communication or information fields to segment their audiences in the service of profitability rather than the public good, we should assume that disparities in access to information will worsen. Such applications are already available in the market place.

'Digital Silhouettes' is the name used by Predictive Networks for one of their products. The resource uses demographics, including race, to characterize Internet consumers' orientations toward 90 content subcategories that are determined on the basis of the firm's analysis of click stream data. Their promotional materials claim that their 'artificial intelligence engine derives individual preferences from web-surfing behavior'. Their promotion claims that 'over time, as more and more sites are visited, the appropriate level of confidence in the accuracy of the Digital Silhouette is established allowing Predictive Networks to accurately model user preferences, affinities and demographics while protecting their privacy' (Predictive Networks, 2001).

While segmentation and targeting may be efficient, and it may serve the competitive and strategic interests of media organizations and their clients, it is also likely to be destructive of the social fabric. Consider the services provided to advertisers by DoubleClick, Inc. DoubleClick identifies itself as a 'Third-party ad service' (Agreement, 2002). DoubleClick 'derives revenue from its ability to record, analyze and target Online Ads based upon User Data, to "help marketers deliver the right message, to the right person, at the right time, while allowing Web publishers to maximize their revenue and build their business in the process"' (Agreement, 2002, p. 5). It is important to note that DoubleClick, and many of its competitors, determines which messages to provide on the basis of data gathered about visits to a host of other Web sites that have little more in common than the fact that they are clients of a particular third-party ad service.

While DoubleClick's primary function is the delivery of advertisements in the Web environment, the same technology, and the same logic, can be used to manage the delivery of editorial content as well (Greening, 2000). This process is at the heart of a kind of self-reinforcing segmentation of the population. Segmentation reinforces difference, while it obscures those things we share in common. This is a point that has been made by Cass Sunstein (2001), in his book, *Republic.com*. Although Sunstein suggests that the increasing polarization we observe is the product of consumer choice, I believe he underestimates the influence of strategic marketing.

It is important to remember that access to information is often determined by the kinds of subsidies that advertisers are willing to provide to publishers in order to gain access to the consumers (and I might add, the voters) whom they value the most. Financial support from advertisers not only provides subsidies to the people who need it least, but by withholding support from media that serve the less desirable audiences, these publishers must either deliver a lower quality product, or seek advertisers with less wholesome commodities for sale. Once again, the differences between us are drawn more sharply, and ironically, they seem to make even more sense because they strengthen the correlations between attributes that actually have no genuinely causal links (Gandy, 2001).

So, what are we to do? The standard responses of governmental agencies like the Federal Trade Commission (FTC) to this sort of discriminatory segmentation are, in my view, unlikely to provide much protection from the dangers that are likely to accompany the widespread use of data mining.

Most recently, the orientation of policy makers in the United States has been toward corporate self-governance, and away from regulation. The FTC has emphasized the value of a much-modified standard of 'fair information practices', which is supposed to ensure that the public enjoys 'notice and choice' regarding the collection and use of personal information.

While consumer-oriented legislation may provide some increased security for individuals in their dealings with the health care establishment, and with regard to their children's exploration of the Web, these regulations are for the most part meaningless as a defence against the social harms that data mining represents.

First of all, the dominant privacy framework is one that emphasizes 'individually identified information'. Although much of the talk in policy circles is about the development and use of consumer profiles, the power of data mining lies not in its ability to target specific individuals, but in its ability to increase the benefits to be derived from controlling the behaviour, on the average, of members of well-defined groups. Individuals increasingly provide a broad range of indexical details that allow decision makers to assign them to the right groups at the right time, in order for a critical decision to be made. List vendors deny that they are targeting individuals when they supply or facilitate the delivery of messages to all the addresses within a defined segment or group.

Second, citizens and consumers cannot expect to be meaningfully informed about the uses to which their transaction-generated information will be applied. This is the case, in part, because even those who manage these data warehouses have only the most general awareness of those future uses. As a result, individuals who encounter tokens of 'notice and choice' really only choose between doing without, and providing an unfettered consent for whatever future uses of information a data manager may discover to be relevant.

In general, consumers somewhat naively believe that their interests are being protected in some way by government regulations that guarantee them access to the information about them being held in some database. The idea is that having this access will enable them to challenge the accuracy of the data that have been recorded in these files. I doubt that there is any meaningful way for an individual consumer to understand, much less challenge, the cumulative score they have been assigned by some data mining operation based on neural net technology.

I recall the classic case of one Claire Cherry, a white woman in Georgia who claimed that she had been a victim of discrimination because Amoco denied her a gasoline credit card. It seems that her application had been denied in part because she lived within a zip code that included a high proportion of African-Americans. The problem that Ms Cherry faced was that the scoring system used by Amoco made use of a multivariate model that included 38 variables. Understandably, she was unable to specify the impact that her zip code, and its underlying racial component, actually had on the determination of her credit status (*Claire Cherry*, 1980). Contemporary scoring models use hundreds of variables and, even more problematic from the perspective of today's consumers, many of these analytical models are adjusted continuously in order to incorporate the latest information that recent transactions provide.

It may be possible for privacy advocates to demand that organizations limit the storage of transaction data for longer than is absolutely necessary (Kang, 1998). They may also attempt to limit the use of this information for purposes unrelated to the initial transaction. This sort of use limitation had been applied to US government agencies in the past, but it seems unlikely, however, that one sector of government would seek the elimination of data in its files at the same time that other sectors are trying to require their secure storage, and increased sharing with any who can claim a legitimate interest. Although the Foreign Intelligence Surveillance Court was extremely critical of the intelligence-sharing proposals of the FBI (United States, 2002), the US Attorney General has enjoyed somewhat more success in gaining acceptance of extended data gathering and sharing between the US and its foreign allies (Scheeres, 2002).

In the final analysis, the best strategies available to those of us who are concerned about the social costs of discrimination may involve the mobilization of public opinion. People tend to be outraged when they discover, or are informed that, they have been discriminated against. There is some value, therefore, in supplying the press with egregious examples of individuals, or communities, or classes of people, who have been victimized by data mining, and by the use of profiles based on irrelevant attributes like race or ethnicity.

On the other hand, it is also likely that the use of data mining in the so-called 'war against terrorists' will soften the public up for its use in a now quiescent war against global competitors, and the threat to shrinking profits. An occasional 'horror story' about some 'so-called victims' of discrimination may do very little to shift the tide of public opinion (Democracy Online Project, 2002; Sullivan, 2001).

4

Joined-up Surveillance: The Challenge to Privacy

Charles D. Raab

'JOINED-UP GOVERNMENT'[1]

The intention of governments to reorient public bureaucracies towards the improved delivery of services to the citizen has resulted in many national and local initiatives for better coordination across a variety of public as well as non-public agencies. This chapter focuses upon recent developments and issues in United Kingdom (UK) government. Diagnosing as an important obstacle the tendency of specific services and their professional and administrative specialists to establish and perform their own routines without regard for cognate specialities, the proponents of reform have criticized the 'silo mentality' of conventional administration. They have offered, instead, a vision of 'joined-up government', in which new attitudes and procedures will be developed, more in keeping with the politically led priority of satisfying citizens' desire for more consistent, more efficient and more effective state services through the use of information and communications technologies (ICTs). ICTs are expected to transform not only 'back-office' processes within agencies, but also relations between the 'front office' and members of the public. One of the main requirements is that personal data be shared among all the organizations that are involved in delivering services. As a surveillance process, however, data-sharing poses problems for the protection of privacy.

These objectives of 'information-age government' (IAG) are valuable and are widely supported. So, too, are other aims associated with public services, including the elimination of fraud and the maintenance of public order. Spatially based policies – for example, efforts to treat certain neighbourhoods comprehensively by bringing together a variety of service

organizations – can also have beneficial effects in line with pro-
gressive social policies. On the other hand, there are dilemmas
inherent in these approaches. Among them, the question of the
impact on personal privacy has gained in prominence in recent
years, although the extent to which privacy as a value can be
reconciled with the objectives of IAG is currently a matter for
policy exploration rather than for the application of ready-made
solutions. We can see IAG in terms of new governance relationships among many organizations that are manoeuvred towards
convergence on the performances involved in the provision of
services, assisted powerfully by the capacity of ICTs to promote
the fulfilment of these objectives.

A UK government White Paper of 1999 illustrated this; it
envisaged linkages between the government's own secure
intranet facilities and public bodies outside of central
government, as well as closer relations between central and local
government and business organizations. Government was
'talking to banks, the Post Office, supermarkets, accountants,
interactive broadcasting companies, the information technology
industry and others about how they can be partners in service
delivery' (UK, Cm 4310, 1999, p. 49). Technology was seen as
helping to 'make it much easier for different parts of government
to work in partnership: central government with local authorities
or the voluntary sector; or government with third-party delivery
channels such as the Post Office or private sector companies'
(UK, Cm 4310, 1999, p. 46).

No one would argue that these objectives could easily be
achieved. The legacy of organizations working separately in the
modern state – even in what is regarded as a unitary administrative system with a unified civil service – is proving to be too
strong for enthusiastically promoted remedies to overcome in a
short time. If this were not so, there would be little reason for
'joined-up government' to be campaigned for as a new aim,
rather than as a summary term for what already exists. Yet in
the UK, problems of consistency in both and policy and implementation have been identified as drawbacks to the provision
of better government. This is especially so when policies and
their implementation take place across the central–local divide,
as they conventionally do in many fields of policy, and when
they are desired to take place with new 'partners' who have

previously stood outside the networks of policy implementation. The implication of new models of 'governance' is that new combinations of policy instruments and organizations can improve upon traditional top-to-bottom approaches. For this effect to happen, new cultures, practices and structures must be brought in, organized around new conceptions of the relationship between the state and the citizen, and designed in conjunction with ICTs. Part of these changes involves some different ways in which government conceives of, and knows, the citizens whom it serves. That knowledge, in turn, is created by novel ways of using information about citizens: collecting, collating, categorizing and communicating personal data within and across the networks of governance.

USING PERSONAL DATA: THE PRIVACY ISSUE

A UK government document has put the general argument, without specific reference only to personal data, that:

> information generated by the statutory and normal workings of government forms the largest single information resource in any developed economy. By making sure the information we hold can be found and passed between the public and private sectors, taking account of privacy and security obligations, we can help to make the most of this asset, thereby driving and stimulating our economy. (UK, Office of the e-Envoy, 2001, p. 3)

This brings the question of privacy into sharper focus, and points up the dilemma of protection. How far can government go in promoting IAG without falling foul of existing laws and practices that have served to limit the dangers to privacy that are posed by information systems and the sharing of data in public services? How can functional, legal, technological and other substitutes be developed to restore, or to go beyond, the protection of privacy that was provided by pre-IAG ways of processing personal information? What new conceptual formulae concerning privacy and joined-up government should be established across the organizations involved with service provision in order to clarify the criteria by which proposed innovations should be judged? Who should be responsible for the machinery that is devised to patrol the boundary between the intensified use and sharing of personal data and the protection of citizens' privacy? Can government and the citizen both 'win', or is 'winning' an inappropriate concept in regard to privacy protection in a joined-up environment of government surveillance? Should IAG policy developments assume that the public is either concerned about, or indifferent to, the privacy implications of new information practices?

These are some of the relevant questions that have formed part of the debate about IAG and privacy in recent years. They have been asked in many countries in which similar policy developments have been in train. In the UK, it has not been easy for government to handle these issues, although in a climate in which privacy may often be disregarded as a relevant value, the recognition that there is a dilemma is an important step towards finding ways of resolving it. An important government report on privacy and data-sharing (UK, Performance and Innovation Unit, Cabinet Office, 2002) grasps this nettle in showing how privacy protection might in practice be placed on a par with data-sharing, thus making good a government commitment to treat privacy as an objective of IAG, and not an obstacle to it. It is true that, where information is a resource in the policy process, its safeguarding within administrative 'silos' may afford a certain level of privacy protection in comparison with the threats posed by a freer interchange of personal data across organizations. Yet privacy protection as a by-product of the fragmented politics of bureaucracy is a stable outcome only if those politics remain the same. IAG changes the politics of bureaucracy towards enhancing the value of the information resource through linkages and wider circulation. Therefore, to remain, at least, at its previous level, privacy protection requires a revamped infrastructure composed of instruments designed to address the special dangers posed by IAG. Thus the trajectory of joined-up government shapes a privacy protection agenda. How likely is it that the latter can be set into motion to match the former?

LAW ENFORCEMENT: SOME ILLUSTRATIONS

Before looking further into this question, these general considerations may be thrown into sharper relief by reference to recent

UK developments in the field of criminal justice and law enforcement, where comprehensive approaches have been proposed.
This field provides useful illustrations of the challenge posed for
privacy protection. The UK government's White Paper (UK, Cm
4310, 1999, pp. 16, 18) emphasized the designing of policy
around shared goals rather than around organizational structures
or existing functions, and this meant coordinated working across
central and local government for a programme of crime
reduction. It also meant coordinated action amongst all agencies
in addressing the drugs problem under the auspices of an Anti-
drugs Co-ordinator, and a joint, holistic approach to planning
and managing the criminal justice system across several
government departments and agencies.

There were already efforts in the 1980s and 1990s to co-
ordinate and even to nationalize electronic information systems
in the police and criminal justice fields (Bellamy & Taylor, 1998,
pp. 56–62), including a Scottish initiative (IScjIS, 1999), although
these have encountered many technical, organizational and
other obstacles. But in another dimension, with specific regard to
computer crime, the National Criminal Intelligence Service
(NCIS) has gone into some detail about how to bring together
resources for combating crime on the information highway. Its
report, Project Trawler (NCIS, 1999a), revealed the limitations of
responses to a range of crimes and issues including computer
hacking, intellectual property offences, fraud, paedophilia and
other criminal communications. Interestingly, a newspaper
commentary on this report attributed these constraints to the
lack of joined-up government among the many police forces and
police organizations, the Home Office and other government
departments in developing a coordinated approach. This would
include the ability to collect and use statistical information that
would show the extent and dimensions of the problem
(Campbell, 1999).

The NCIS report's inventory of participants and strategies for
a better response is worth seeing as an illustration of a very comprehensive strategy; it included the following:

- Legislation (protection for trade secrets; strengthen
  Computer Misuse Act; 'lawful access to decryption keys (in
  prescribed circumstances)')

- Internet users (taking technical security precautions; reporting to police and the Internet Watch Foundation; forming self-help groups; audit logs; filtering and rating)
- Customers ('first bastion against fraud')
- Industry (investigations; lawsuits; self-regulation; technical solutions; cooperating with law enforcement)
- Companies and industry-wide organisations (Internet traders protecting trade marks; monitoring for criminal developments and letting law enforcement know)
- Software and audio industry trade associations (prosecutions; publicity; educating end-users; hotlines for the public; rewarding 'whistleblowers'; in-store inspections)
- Market forces (self-regulation of gambling and adult pornography; international self-regulatory body to establish trustworthy sites, monitor for compliance, and warn the customer; cooperating with law enforcement)
- Technical solutions (biometrics; fraud screening software; e-mail filters; digital watermarks; cryptography and digital signatures to authenticate identities)
- Police forces (take action; training and awareness)
- Law enforcement regulators (monitoring, interception and seizure of illicit goods; surveillance of extremists, hackers and phreakers)
- National intelligence ('single dedicated national unit' to determine priorities for action, investigate serious crimes; 'centre of excellence' for cybercrime issues; support local forces; inspire public confidence; international liaison; improve coordination and make economies)
- Publicity (for successful law enforcement)
- International cooperation (harmonize legislation and policy; combined operations; standardization of techniques; extradition; information exchange)
- Law enforcement-industry links (raise public awareness; promote best practice; develop counter-crime tools; get ISPs' expertise and lawful access to subscriber information on board).

The project report thus had a keen sense of the variety of strategic actors and instruments that are necessary for a holistic approach:

combating crime is not simply a matter for Government and law enforcement. The IT industry, Internet infrastructure firms, corporate and private users, and the media have responsibilities and a role to play too. Indeed, such are the dynamics and pace of change of the 'IT world' that some users and businesses will be far ahead of law enforcement in identifying measures to prevent and detect crime. (NCIS, 1999a, para. 103)

In the inventory's elaborate array, there were many indications of how different strategies and participants can join together in combating computer crime. NCIS used the concept of 'partnership' to refer to links between law enforcement and industry – the public and the private sector – and to international action. This ambitious strategic approach was inspired by NCIS's desire to preside over a comprehensive law enforcement approach, at least in one country. The long development of the facility for cross-border police cooperation, including the information systems, that is provided in Europe under the Schengen Agreement on the abolition of common border controls and under Europol, illustrates the arduous and troubled process of creating more joined-up policing on the international level (Anderson et al., 1995). Nevertheless NCIS, which houses the UK's Interpol and Europol National Criminal Bureaux, saw itself as a 'one-stop-shop' that would include the functions of the UK's national Schengen Information System (SIRENE Bureau – Supplementary Information Request at the National Entry under the UK's participation in the expanded Schengen arrangements (NCIS, 1998, 1999b).

With regard to initiatives illustrated by Project Trawler, the question is whether privacy protection is in danger of losing out to a more holistic and joined-up system of law enforcement, which, in combating 'cyber' crime, may seriously invade privacy. Perhaps especially in the world of policing and criminal justice, many exemptions from the rules governing breaches of privacy have claimed justification on the grounds of overriding public interest. In any case, if the question is whether privacy protection requires a commensurate strategy to match the threats posed by many of these tools, then, in the world of data protection, there may be fewer possibilities and resources for such an entrepreneurial approach, especially given the perception that privacy protection is less of a burning issue than fighting crime.

A contrasting illustration in the field of law enforcement is UK legislation concerning crime and disorder. The Crime and Disorder Act 1998 deals with antisocial behaviour, sex offences, child safety, child curfews, parenting, noisy neighbours, truanting, racially aggravated assaults, and much more. The partnership schemes to be developed amongst local agencies will have a large scope, including drug misuse, domestic violence, football-related disorder, the activities of Neighbourhood Watch, and so on. There is the potential for a great deal of information exchange among local councils, the police, and health authorities, which might be very effective in combating crime and disorder. However, when coupled with the wide interpretation of 'disorder' or 'antisocial behaviour', and the very large number of provisions of the Act, it could be the gateway to a substantial invasion of privacy and the civil liberties of the individual. For instance, Section 115 of the Act, on Disclosure of Information, says:

(1) Any person who, apart from this subsection, would not have power to disclose information –
(a) to a relevant authority; or
(b) to a person acting on behalf of such an authority, shall have power to do so in any case where the disclosure is necessary or expedient for the purposes of any provision of this Act. (UK, Home Office 1999)

This is very wide; it relates to 'any provision' of the Act – which itself is very comprehensive – and leaves a lot to the judgement of what is 'necessary or expedient'.

Information is essential to achieving the aims of the Act. But the policy stipulates that there must be rules and explicit, agreed and transparent procedures that govern the extent to which information is used and shared. This underlines the importance of the Data Protection Act 1998 as well as the protocols developed between police forces and the other authorities. In this departure, there is an attempt to introduce explicit privacy safeguards for the integration of information about identifiable individuals, by means of agreed protocols among the police and other agencies involved. The Information Commissioner has given relevant advice; so, too, has the Home Office. A joint statement by the Information Commissioner (then called the Data Protection Registrar) and the Home Office concerning crime and disorder partnerships (UK, Home Office, 1998) pointed out that the police have a common law power to disclose information for the prevention and detection of crime. Other public bodies might not have had power to disclose information to the police or to other bodies before the Disorder Act gave it to them. But the Act does not give them the obligation to disclose; therefore, the Data Protection Act and other common law provisions (such as the duty of confidence) govern those disclosures. The statement said that the Data Protection Act's Principles are extremely important. They require that personal information should be collected and processed fairly and lawfully, disclosed only in appropriate circumstances, be accurate, relevant and up-to-date, not be held for longer than is necessary for the purpose, be kept securely, and also be accessible and correctable by the individual concerned.

As the joint statement noted, the public:

> rightly expects that personal information known to public bodies will be properly protected. However, the public also expects the proper sharing of information, as this can be an important weapon against crime. Agencies should, therefore, seek to share information where this would be in the public interest. (UK, Home Office, 1998)

One could argue that this puts great pressure on those who collect and hold the information, and catches them in the middle of competing legal and policy requirements and expectations. They have to make decisions and 'balancing' judgements based upon these competing pressures. Local authorities, perhaps especially housing departments, might want a lot of information from the police, but the police may be reluctant to exchange more than the minimum necessary, and the Data Protection Act might support the police's view.

In any case, the Information Commissioner has pointed out that the Crime and Disorder Act 'does not entitle the relevant agencies or authorities to enter into wholesale data-sharing or matching. Any initiative set up under the auspices of the Act must be aimed at reducing crime or the fear of crime' (Information Commissioner, n.d.). A similar issue arose in 1998 with regard to another area of law enforcement policy: the combating of social security fraud. When some UK local authorities demanded the wholesale disclosure of staff payroll information from local employers including supermarkets, a brewery, and the Post Office, they were warned that it was a mistake to believe that they had a automatic right to this information so that they could run sets of data against each other to detect possible fraudsters. A similar danger could arise under the Crime and Disorder Act, but for the safeguards that are supposed to be erected for regulating the sharing of data.

The Home Office has produced extensive and detailed guidance on the partnerships to be developed under the Act (UK, Home Office, 1999). One chapter dealt with information exchange, and went further than the joint statement. It drew attention to the need to establish the existence of legal powers to disclose information, and to the need to see that such disclosure is done on a proper basis with due regard to common and statute law, including the duty of confidence and the Data Protection Principles. It observed that, under the Data Protection Act, there are exemptions available for the non-disclosure rules where failure to disclose would be likely to prejudice crime-prevention or -detection objectives. But in the request for disclosure – for example, where a housing department wants information held by the police in order to bring a civil proceeding against a tenant – the agency needs to specify why the information is necessary to the success of the proceedings, and why the proceedings, if successful, would prevent crime. The Commissioner and the Home Office have argued that the best way forward is by means of protocols between the information-sharing agencies at local level, in which the rules can be carefully specified. One of the benefits in establishing such protocols may well be the educative effect on all those concerned, in terms of a better appreciation of the uses and limits of personal information, and the advantages for combating crime and disorder. But in addition, the process of devising protocols opens up for discussion the risks posed to privacy, and the ways in which concepts like the 'public interest' and the 'balance' between crime control and privacy protection can be thought about in practice when officials are faced with difficult judgements and decisions about the proper extent and manner of surveillance.

The Commissioner has provided a checklist to guide the setting-up of information-sharing arrangements and protocols, indicating the way in which privacy safeguards can, in principle, be devised to match the potential dangers posed by joined-up ways of controlling crime and disorder. The checklist asks:

(i)   What is the purpose of the information-sharing arrangements?
(ii)   Will it be necessary to share personal information in order to fulfil that purpose?
(iii) Do the parties to the arrangement have the power to disclose personal information for that purpose?
(iv)   How much personal information will need to be shared in order to achieve the objectives of the arrangement?
(v)   Should the consent of the individual be sought before disclosure is made?
(vi)   What if the consent of the individual is not sought, or has been sought but is withheld?
(vii) How does the non-disclosure exemption apply?
(viii) How do you ensure compliance with the other data protection principles?

THREE CONCEPTIONS OF PRIVACY PROTECTION

Further afield from the area of law enforcement, the value of privacy is in fact seen as of growing importance for those who are concerned that public trust in the processes of electronic commerce and electronic government be created and maintained (Raab, 1998). International bodies such as the European Commission as well as national governments and the private sector have taken this point on board. A large number of official documents as well as public pronouncements by leading government and industry figures say that trust is the indispensable prerequisite in an online world. Therefore, in recent years a conventional wisdom has developed that privacy protection, whether in an online environment or offline, requires a mixed strategy of privacy instruments that includes internationally agreed principles, national and sectoral laws, self-regulation through voluntary codes of practice, privacy-enhancing technologies, market solutions, citizen or consumer education and individual self-protection, and other devices (Raab, 1997; Reidenberg, 1997).

An elaboration of this framework cannot be undertaken here (see Bennett & Raab, 2003). However, to some extent the flexibility of this array of instruments, and their configuration in a variety of mutually supportive combinations, may constitute an attempt to enhance privacy protection in number of environments. These include not only electronic commerce and private-sector relationships between companies and their customers, but also electronic government and state-citizen transactions as well. It is the latter that is of especial interest in recent UK developments within the IAG initiative as a whole. To an extent, the 1999 White Paper's multi-faceted privacy strategy reflected this approach. It pledged that the government would:

- work closely with the [Information Commissioner] to ensure that privacy implications of electronic service delivery are fully addressed.
- carry through our commitment to openness, so that the citizen has relevant information about our initiatives as they are developed and implemented.
- promote specific codes of practice, on a departmental or inter-departmental basis, for information age government.
- benefit from the [Information Commissioner's] powers to conduct independent assessments of the processing of personal data.
- Deploy privacy-enhancing technologies, so that data is disclosed, accessed or identified with an individual only to the extent necessary.
- provide a proper and lawful basis for data sharing where this is desirable, for example in the interest of improved service or fraud reduction consistent with our commitment to protect privacy. (UK, Cm 4310, 1999, p. 51)

Although the momentum for joined-up government has arguably slowed over the past year or so, the report on privacy and data-sharing (UK, Performance and Innovation Unit, Cabinet Office, 2002) includes a fairly elaborate set of proposals for policy and practice, which, if implemented, might provide a credible infrastructure for privacy protection in the midst of surveillance using personal data for – among other things – combating fraud. This would arbitrate the terms and conditions on which the delivery of public services is carried out in a climate in which public trust and confidence in government, and in its ability to safeguard privacy, cannot be taken for granted. To understand the shaping of this infrastructure, it is useful to identify three alternative conceptions of the relationship between privacy and IAG that can be found in the UK discourse on these matters (Raab, 2001). These are that:

- privacy is a barrier to joined-up government and service provision because it restricts the exploitation of personal data for these purposes;
- it is the lack of privacy that forms the barrier because it interferes with the trust and confidence that people must have for IAG transactions to take place;
- privacy protection is not just a means to the other ends of IAG, but is one of its intrinsic objectives.

Without further research in depth, it is too simple to map these positions onto distinctive interests, coalitions or networks within the policy circles in which these are important matters for decision, although the positions do not appear to be randomly distributed across these milieux. It may also be too simple to argue that there has been a shift from consensus on the first position to consensus on the second, and then to the third. As mentioned earlier, the 'trust and confidence' argument has gained prominence as conventional wisdom and as a guide to policy for information superhighways and the transactions that are hoped to take place along them. An alternative argument, however, would be that, over the years, there has been a discernible contest between proponents of the first two, perhaps especially across different policy domains and functions of the state. The conflict between commercial interests and law enforcement interests over the establishment of secure electronic commerce – in the UK, played out over the passage of the Electronic Communication Act 2000 – has illustrated the different ecologies of interest. Thus the controversy over cryptography was very largely about business's need to safeguard the security and confidentiality of information in electronic transactions, as against the need for law enforcement agencies to have access to the contents of these communications.

The third position has come into the contest as a relatively new contender. The formation of ICT and infrastructural requisites for IAG has proceeded over the past years since the government first set forward its electronic government programme vision in a 1996 paper (UK, Cm 3438, 1996), and in a host of documents and development reports since then (Raab, 2001). Within this sequence, the third position was, in fact, clearly enunciated in the 1999 White Paper, which said:

> There is concern that information technology could lead to mistaken identity, inadvertent disclosure and inappropriate transfer of data. The Government will address these concerns and will demonstrate our belief that *data protection is an objective of information age government, not an obstacle to it.* (UK, Cm 4310, 1999, p. 51; emphasis in original)

This is a significant recognition, an encouraging step in the direction of privacy protection within the state; as mentioned earlier, it has been reinforced in governmental proposals for data-sharing (UK, Performance and Innovation Unit, Cabinet Office, 2002). However, its robustness remains to be demonstrated in the further implementation of governmental plans for sharing personal data, in part for law enforcement purposes. The extent to which such implementation can live with such a conceptual-ization is still not clear.

A rhetorical reconciliation of the dual objectives may not easily withstand the pressure of policy imperatives for greater surveil-lance. It is likely to be difficult to specify agreed criteria by which the achievement of the objective of privacy can be judged, although that is not a new problem in the world of privacy protection. More importantly, perhaps, it may not be possible to provide a reasoned discrimination among the different levels of privacy that may be desirable or necessary in different parts of IAG – assuming of course, that 'levels' can be measured (Raab & Bennett, 1996). On the other hand, if the privacy risks of mistaken identity, inadvertent disclosure and inappropriate transfer of data are taken as some of the major operational foci of the third conception when translated into practical policy, then, it could be argued, the privacy objective would be to reduce these risks to some pre-specified targets – assuming, of course, that risks can be measured. But this approach might simply shift the terms of controversy, rather than settle it.

The problem of ascertaining 'levels' of privacy notwithstanding, the three conceptions point in different directions in terms of the extent and characteristics of privacy protection that each one legitimates and sustains. For example, if the first is preferred, only a minimum level of protection might be called for, consistent with compliance with statutory and common law provisions, and with the requirements of the physical security of data. If the second, then a more careful tailoring of a higher level of protection might be indicated, sufficient to sustain public confidence and trust commensurate with a designated rate of development of electronic service transactions. Since that development has been mandated to become very high over the next few years, the prospects for greater privacy protection should be good. If, however, privacy protection is an objective in its own right, then one might expect a more vigorous championing of privacy against possible abuses of personal data. This might perhaps be done through special monitoring and implementation machinery, and through a more thoroughgoing reformation of the administrative culture even within the more complex joined-up governmental environment. It may also be attempted through the development of specific incentives and sanctions, within public organizations and among them, to govern the processing and exchange of data. Protocols, transparency tools, codes of practice, and pledges or commitments to the public may be among the non-technological vehicles for implementing the third conception.

In a sense, we may say that the three conceptions form a ladder of privacy protection, not so much in spurious quantitative terms, but in terms of the substantive kinds of change that must be leveraged throughout the networks of organizations and instruments that shape the protection of privacy. But it may be difficult, or unrealistic, to expect all parts of the public sector to ascend the ladder at the same pace; in other words, the vehicles mentioned above may be unevenly developed across the board. Agencies vary in their legacy of systems and cultures for processing personal data, in their functional requirements for the use or disclosure of those data, and in their outlooks on how far and how fast they can effect change in the direction of better privacy protection. Therefore, there are different ladders, rather than one broad staircase up which all parts of the state should be expected to travel in unison. The difficulty is that joined-up privacy protection may actually require a 'staircase' approach rather than a collection of 'ladders', and policy implementation in the UK towards this is occurring through centrally orchestrated innovation in practices, role development and technologies for privacy in IAG. This is precisely because, if joined-up, information-age government means that personal data should flow across the various organizations that are involved together in providing a particular set of citizen services, then the data should not move through zones of differential risks of privacy violation. To change the metaphor, the canal along which the data travel should not require locks. In this sense, the problems of creating joined-up data protection in IAG can be viewed as a microcosm of those that have been involved in transborder data flows at the global or international level, where questions of equivalence or adequacy have been the mainstay of policy debate, international negotiation and legislation. None of the three conceptions of privacy in IAG can escape these issues within the confines of a single state.

The different sets of expectations that arise from the three positions cannot be pursued here in any depth, but they can be used as rough benchmarks for looking at UK policy formation, particularly with regard to one of the main implications of IAG for privacy that has been outlined: the sharing of personal data across organizational boundaries. The private sector has pioneered techniques to extract the maximum commercially valuable information from the data that can be obtained about actual or potential customers. Beyond the law enforcement illustrations given earlier, the public sector is pursuing something similar. For instance, there are developments in information systems for combating and clearing up crime through sophisticated, forensic-led crime analytic systems employing geo-spatially coded data about suspects, victims, crimes, and so on. But there are also important initiatives for the more efficient processing of personal data in order to serve citizens better when they transact a host of dealings with the state, both mandatory and elective. These IAG initiatives in the UK are complex and not yet clearly successful, although on a small scale or pilot basis there have been promising signs. One policy aim is to avoid needless and irritating duplication of information requests made to individual members of the public for registering their changes in personal status, for claiming their entitlements to services and benefits, for applying for necessary documents, and for other purposes. The accuracy, sufficiency and timeliness of personal data are to be improved, and better common data standards are to be adopted. None of these are necessarily antithetical to good privacy protection, and may in fact help to realize it.

The problems, however, include the difficulty of agreeing on the limits to which collections of data can be shared or matched beyond their original purpose if the public policy purposes seem legitimate. There are many legitimate aims within a liberal-democratic system of government that has a large public sector. Among these are better services, combating fraud in the welfare state, promoting law and order, targeting programmes either geographically or socially, promoting new ways of teamworking for health and social care, and integrating processes across the disparate, but mutually functioning, institutions of the criminal justice system. Achieving some of these aims in the UK may involve applications of ICT that require special, but very controversial, social innovations such as identity cards and the apparatus of authentication and verification of individuals and their entitlements. If so, then public apprehension about what happens to personal information, or about what may be perceived as surveillance, may become an important factor arbitrating success or failure. The third conception of the place of privacy in IAG may be more difficult to achieve, depending on, for instance, the precise nature and privacy implications of the technologies that are brought into play. But there are many other issues involved in the sharing of data in the public sector, not the least of which is the quality of the data that are shared (UK, Office of the e-Envoy, 2001). This has implications for the effectiveness and efficiency of these plans, but also for adherence to several of the relevant data protection principles. In addition, on the research side as well as the clinical side of health care, the vexed question of informed consent, perhaps especially where disease registers are involved, has been a matter of great debate.

A crucial prerequisite of IAG is public trust in the way in which their data are dealt with. Government may be trying to lift itself up by its bootstraps when it seeks to increase this aspect of public trust, given the relatively low degree of trust in government in general that seems to prevail. In addition, increasing the level of trust in information-dependent transactions may only partly involve improving privacy protection as such. This may be particularly true if it is the accuracy and efficiency of data-handling, and the convenience and speed of service-related transactions, that are perceived as the factors that are more likely to encourage the public, and if those factors entail a privacy trade-off. In this sense, we may only be at the level of the second conception of privacy rather than the third, at least until we can understand better what the public values, and whether they see privacy protection as an intrinsic part of a properly functioning IAG, rather than as an optional extra to be taken in small doses, or as an obstacle to what they really want from these transactions. The proportion of the public that fears the privacy effects of data-sharing may be significant, although there is only patchy research evidence of that so far.[2]

However, we may be within the scope of the third conception if we understand that the technical reliability of data networks, as well as the improvement of verification and authentication methods and the assignment of legal liability, contribute to trust and to the protection of privacy.

Given the prominence of privacy-enhancing technologies (PETs) in the current armoury of instruments for data protection, it is likely that IAG data-sharing will heavily involve the use of tools such as smartcards, encryption, identification numbers, biometric devices and other mechanisms for authentication (UK, Cm 5557, 2002). There has already been a good deal of development work under way, but the precise configuration of these technologies and their infrastructures will be crucial in determining whether they enhance privacy or merely settle for a lesser degree of protection compatible with the aim of streamlining the public services. These are politically sensitive issues at the best of times; as the conclusion to this chapter implies, this may not be the best of times. Raising the profile of PETs just when the issue of personal identification has become overlain with considerations of national security may require policy management of a high order if only to satisfy the requirements of the second rung on the ladder of privacy conceptions.

If the attempt to combine data-sharing with privacy protection embraces a variety of instruments – management procedures, laws, self-regulation, PETs, and others – in an integrated, rather than piecemeal and fragmented, strategy across the public sector, then we may be able to say that joined-up government has been paralleled by data protection that is joined-up in two dimensions: across organizations, and across privacy instruments. Whether these elements can extend to the private sector in its public-service delivery roles is a question for another time.

CONCLUSION: PRIVACY AND DATA-SHARING IN A TIME OF CRISIS

It may be especially difficult to invoke privacy considerations, or indeed to launch new joined-up initiatives in a climate of perceived crisis that seems to require enhanced surveillance through more intensive gathering and collating of information and intelligence. Global anti-terrorist activities have gained the upper hand in the aftermath of the September 11, 2001 terrorist attacks on the US. What might have come to be regarded as protected databases may be rendered accessible through the exercise of old or new legal powers. For example, the UK's Anti-terrorism, Crime and Security Act, passed in December 2001, brings down the barrier to information-sharing among organizations. The providers of communication services must retain personal data beyond their own requirements so that they can be available, not only for purposes of national security, but for broader law enforcement purposes under the Regulation of Investigatory Powers Act 2000, which may have nothing to do with the security of the state. These measures revise settlements of the 'security versus privacy' debate that have been achieved with considerable difficulty over the past few years, and may change the nature of the trade-off between privacy and other values that takes place in domains remote from the current climate of insecurity. The UK Information Commissioner has expressed her concern over the potential of these powers:

> There is no evidence of the slackening of the pace or the weakening of the resolve of those who wish to take forward law enforcement initiatives. It is the important task of the data protection community to make sure that those measures that

impact on privacy are a proportionate and effective response to the menace that they seek to combat. (UK, House of Commons, 2002, p. 19)

There has thus been a movement back in the direction of the lowest rung on the ladder – the first conception of the place of privacy – in the ascendancy of security agendas in and among countries. New immunities from privacy protection have been found for the flow of personal data, not only in the pursuit of anti-terrorist goals, but in ancillary activities that give evidence of 'function creep' (Foundation for Information Policy Research, 2001). The development of techniques for protecting privacy in the everyday world of joined-up public services may appear to some to be a luxury that leans too far in the direction of the transparent, citizen-friendly and often consented sharing of personal information. Whether that world can be insulated from heavier surveillance approaches responding to a different agenda, even in the public interest, cannot be foretold. Civil liberties, of which privacy may be one, are often suspended during wartime or other periods of actual or perceived threat to political institutions. The momentum of the third conception of privacy may be slowed or reversed if the attentions of central policy-makers are distracted from such innovations that might place limits on the sharing of data. The pressure of other policy considerations may affect the shaping of specific processes, including technologies for sharing data and protecting privacy. It may also seriously restrict the scope for privacy commissioners and other regulators to intervene. But the likelihood of any of these uncomfortable expectations coming to fruition is difficult to estimate without further research investigation. Meanwhile, in the current crisis, it is not easy to separate rumour from fact in the welter of scenarios that are offered on all sides.

NOTES

1. I am grateful to the Rathenau Institute for having given me the opportunity to present an earlier version of this chapter at the Conference on Privacy held under their auspices in Amsterdam, January 17, 2002.
2. See the research conducted by MORI and Perri 6 in UK, Performance and Innovation Unit, Cabinet Office (2002), Annex C, available at http://www.piu.gov.uk/2002/privacy/report/annex-c.htm.

5
'They Don't Even Know We're There': The Electronic Monitoring of Offenders in England and Wales[1]

Mike Nellis

INTRODUCTION

The electronic monitoring (EM) of offenders, colloquially known as 'tagging',[2] was piloted experimentally under the last Conservative government but only became a nationwide provision under New Labour. Unlike mainland Europe, where probation services have accommodated EM with varying degrees of enthusiasm and resistance (Whitfield, 2001), it is delivered in Britain by a range of private sector organizations who, though regulated by the Home Office, seemingly have little managerial or operational contact with probation or youth justice services. It is thus a parallel rather than an integrated development – even when the same individual offender is subject to both EM and a rehabilitative programme. Each phase of EM's operational development has been well researched by the Home Office but 'despite being one of the most innovative developments of the decade' (Windelsham, 2001, p. 292) criminological theorists have shown little interest in it: it simply 'grew incrementally on the fringes of penal policy, attracting relatively little attention and diminishing antagonism' (ibid.). This chapter will contend that the growth of EM is a more significant development in British criminal justice than has generally been recognized and, whilst accepting that it could and should have a place in the repertoire of responses to crime, fears that it is highly likely to have a transformative and deleterious effect on the field of community penalties. As the Institute of Criminology (Bottoms, Gelsthorpe & Rex 2001) noted in a colloquium on the future of such penalties, its actual use is already outstripping our capacity to think through its significance, let alone guide its development; the potential of both the technology and the private sector providers has been underestimated. A monitoring officer once proudly said to me, whilst demonstrating a hand-held device used for the discreet drive-by monitoring of an offender's home or workplace, 'they don't even know we're there' (personal communication, September 23, 2001). For criminologists, this is almost true in a metaphoric sense, too.

Focusing on the English probation service, this chapter will appraise the past, and speculate on the future, dividing the period under consideration into four phases. The first phase reflects great wariness towards EM – *rebuttal* – which was initially successful, eventually less so. The current phase, established after some credibility had been won for EM, is aptly described as *supplementary* (an uneasy coexistence of EM and probation) – and cogent arguments have been put to ensure that, in all essentials, give or take a little refinement, developments should rest here (Whitfield, 1997; 2001). I will argue, however, because of the highly managerialized context in which EM is developing, that a *displacement* phase (EM becoming the defining, normal element of community supervision) is quite likely, and that a *supercession* phase (EM providers becoming a more dominant force in offender management than probation) is certainly possible – not least because New Labour has shown itself lukewarm towards the probation service, and favourably disposed towards commercial involvement in the public sector in general, and criminal justice in particular. This sequence is at least rendered plausible by the insights of Gary Marx (1988) and David Lyon (2001a), into the emergence of late modern 'surveillance societies' and by what can arguably be characterized as an emerging shift in the community penalty field from a humanistic to a surveillant paradigm.

ELECTRONIC MONITORING 1981–99

In its modern operational form, both the *idea* and *practice* of EM developed first in the US, the period of conception to first trial (in New Mexico) lasting from 1977 to 1982 (Fox, 1987). It was not until 1989–90 that it was tried in Britain, largely as a result of lobbying by the Offender Tag Association (founded in 1981/82 by journalist and prison visitor Tom Stacey), which drew the government's attention to American developments (Stacey, 1989; 1993; see also Nellis, 2001), and also because of the known interest of some companies in the security and telecommunications business (Chubb and Marconi). Stacey's ideal was always a form of *tracking* tagging (following offenders' movements), but he accepted that in the 1980s the available technology made possible only curfew tagging (restricting offenders to a specific location, usually their home). The Conservative government was initially dismissive of the idea, but its 'punishment in the community' initiative (1988–92), aiming to reduce custody by toughening community penalties, provided the pretext for the first experiment with EM in Britain. A group of politicians and civil servants visited some American schemes and were sufficiently impressed to authorize an experiment here. To avoid complex legislative debate, which would have arisen if *sentenced* offenders had been focused upon, defendants at risk of remand in custody (pre-trial detention) were selected. A brief scheme in three adult courts tagged only 50 adult bailees in a 12-month period, some of whom absconded and/or reoffended, and who also received a disproportionate amount of media attention because of the novelty of the measure to which they were subjected.

The introduction of EM in Britain was deeply controversial, at least among those concerned with administering community penalties. It was initially opposed by liberal penal reform groups and the probation service as an unwelcome Orwellian intrusion into criminal justice. The Howard League, in response to the government Green Paper in which it was first proposed, claimed that it was 'incompatible with the essential fabric of a free society' (1988, p. 5). The Quaker Penal Affairs Committee stated flatly that 'the degradation by electronic monitoring of fellow human beings is morally wrong' (quoted in Allchin, 1989, p. 819). The National Association for the Care and Rehabilitation of Offenders (Nacro), the Prison Reform Trust, and the Penal Affairs Consortium all mounted a mix of practical and political arguments against it. Magistrates collectively seemed unimpressed, although there were individual exceptions (Berg, 1996). Both liberal and conservative newspapers were sceptical of its

potential either to reduce crime or to reduce the use of imprisonment, but grudgingly acknowledged that it should be given a
chance to prove its worth. It was generally seen to threaten the
humanistic traditions that had historically informed penal
reform and social work and, specifically in the case of probation,
to encroach on its professional territory. The National Association of Probation Officers (NAPO) – a professional
association/trade union – began an active campaign against it,
ensuring that EM got bad publicity. The Association of Chief
Officers of Probation (ACOP) – the probation managers' organization – was, at least to begin with, equally hostile.

Resistance of this kind possibly did impede its development in
England and Wales, and, although, a Curfew Order with
Electronic Monitoring was authorized in the Criminal Justice Act
1991, for 16 year olds and above, for periods of six months
maximum, the Home Office showed no *overt* interest in implementing it. Napo confidently believed that EM had been
abandoned, but in the context of much-toughened public and
political attitudes towards law and order after 1993, and a significant shift to the Right within the Conservative government,
a new Home Secretary, deeply hostile to the probation service,
activated the dormant idea of curfew orders. He implemented it
experimentally in three counties (later seven), quite explicitly
without regard for the possibility of it reducing prison use.[3] This
firm indication that government was determined to press on
with EM forced those opposed to it to reconsider their position,
and perhaps to reflect more deeply on what it took to create
credible community penalties. ACOP adapted first, recognizing,
partly on the basis of American evidence, that it could be used
constructively in conjunction with rehabilitative programmes,
and Swedish experience that it could reduce the need for prison
places, and that it would be better to be on the inside of
government debates about the use of EM than to remain aloof,
hostile and without influence. Frontline probation officers
remained sceptical for longer, and Napo's emphasis switched
from moralistic arguments against tagging (which it felt had been
lost, or had limited purchase) to cost-effectiveness arguments. It
looked, with some optimism, towards the prospect of a New
Labour government in 1997, because in opposition New Labour
had seemed, despite a generally tough stance on crime, to at least

be ambivalent about EM,[4] and hostile to the privatization of prisons. Napo's optimism proved misplaced, on both counts.

ELECTRONIC MONITORING SINCE 1999

It was under New Labour that EM moved from experimental status in Britain to being a measure available to all courts. Curfew orders were rolled out nationally in December 1999, but continuing low take-up – only 4000 were made in the first year – meant that relatively few criminal justice personnel or offenders experienced tagging. Curfew orders were soon surpassed by New Labour's own contribution to EM – the Home Detention Curfew scheme (HDC), which it introduced nationally in January 1999 without prior experimentation. It entailed early release from prison for short-sentence prisoners (adults aged 18 and above, with a curfew period not exceeding 60 days). Fourteen thousand releases were made in the first year. The lack of experimentation indicated a desperate government need to create a safety valve for managing the rising prison population. Although only one-third of prisoners eligible for release passed satisfactory risk assessments, the number of offenders subject to electronic monitoring has been greater with HDC than with any other measure, and has massively increased the business of the monitoring companies. Reoffending was minimal, although such as there was was exploited by the political opposition, and by victims groups, to criticize the very principle of early release.[5] Nonetheless, after a positive appraisal by the Prison and Probation Inspectorates in 2001, the Home Secretary requested its further use (making it presumptive rather than discretionary, extending the curfew period to 90 days), urgently pressing ahead with this after the prison population in England passed 70,000 in February 2002. Prison governors – with whom discretion about release rests – had been ambivalent about the HDC scheme, partly because it entailed considerable work (collating risk assessment information) with the kind of short-sentence prisoners who are increasingly thought of (even by prison governors) as inappropriately sentenced to prison.

The Crime (Sentences) Act 1997 had permitted the extension of curfew orders to younger juveniles (10–15 year olds, with a three-month maximum curfew), but New Labour did not implement this until February 2001.[6] This made possible, in April 2001, the creation of 50 Intensive Supervision and Surveillance Programmes (ISSPs), run by local Youth Offending Teams, for the 3 per cent (N = 2500) of persistent young offenders deemed responsible for 25 per cent of all crime (Bateman, 2001). The programmes, which *could* last for up to six months, were made available at three points in the youth justice process: as conditions in supervision or probation orders, as part of the community element of a Detention and Training Order (a prototype seamless sentence, mixing both custodial and community-based elements), or as part of a bail supervision scheme. They subject young offenders to 25 hours' compulsory education per week in the first three months of the programme, and encourage reparation, as well as using electronic monitoring (including voice verification technology), and mentoring 'to ensure young people are in the right place at the right time' (George, 2002, p. 25). It was hoped that the sophisticated 'surveillance and monitoring' (which also includes intelligence-led policing) would 'provide reassurance to communities' (ibid.). The intensity of support and surveillance diminishes in the second three months, and any supervision or probation order can continue after the ISSP has ended.

Between April and June 2002 EM was again piloted as an adjunct to bail – but only for selected young offenders, age 12–16. Under the Criminal Justice and Police Act 2002 unconvicted suspects on bail were made eligible for tagging if magistrates considered them at risk of offending. There were numerous reasons behind this. It aimed to prevent reoffending whilst on bail, but it also relieved manifest pressure on secure and custodial accommodation in the childcare and penal systems respectively. The pilots took place in ten large regions in which the government's 'street crime initiative' had been operational, and were then rolled out nationally.

In addition to these existing uses in Britain, other uses have been anticipated and, indeed, legislated for. The Criminal Justice and Court Services Act 2000 permitted the electronic monitoring of *any requirement* of a community penalty (at the court's discretion) – in essence making EM integral to the very nature of community penalties – as well as a curfew order, and the newly proposed exclusion order. This latter disposal requires an offender to stay away from certain places at certain times, and is aimed at offenders who pose a nuisance or a danger to particular victims (who are given alarms sensitive to the tag worn by the offender). Like curfews, it can be used as a stand-alone penalty, or in conjunction with rehabilitation programmes. The Act also made provision for EM to be imposed where offenders are released from custody, not 'early' (as in HDC) but at their official release date – in essence making EM integral to all post-release supervision, including that of lifers. It anticipates the coming of tracking technology (possibly using satellites)[7] and establishes the power of the Home Secretary 'to monitor electronically *the movements* of such offenders whilst subject to post release supervision' (Home Office, 2000, p. 7 emphasis added). All these measures were to be piloted, but their implementation was delayed, and take-up has been slight

There has also been speculation about the future of tagging, not just in terms of new technologies such as GPS (which is one way of enabling tracking) but also in terms of offender categories that are particularly suitable. Released sex offenders (a group about whom there is regular public/media concern) are continually spoken of in this respect, although such has been the severity of the alarm about them that, having initially been eligible for HDC, they were subsequently excluded from it. Nonetheless, tracking tagged sex offenders during some of the extended supervision period (English law allows up to 10 years) continues to surface in debate, although no concrete plans have been made. Even Harry Fletcher of NAPO has conceded that in this respect 'a stricter use of electronic tagging ... would make a vast difference in preventing reoffending' (www.news.bbc.co.uk December 13, 2001).

PUBLIC DEBATE AND ELECTRONIC MONITORING

Home Office research has made available considerable amounts of data on the operational aspects of tagging, including its minor technical imperfections, on sentencers' attitudes towards its use, on inter-agency aspects of its administration at local level, and on its impact on curfewees. The slow take-up of curfew orders can largely be attributed to magistrates', probation officers' and youth offending teams' lack of confidence in them, partly occasioned by poor knowledge, poor training and disputes among themselves as to the appropriate hours offenders should be curfewed (Walter, Sugg & Moore, 2001). Home Detention Curfew, despite its initially lower than expected take-up, was soon deemed cost-effective (Dodgson et al., 2001). As their knowledge of EM increased, sceptics' (especially probation officers) sense of its potential has grown (Nellis & Lilly, 2000) and practitioners themselves seem to be concluding that it is underused (Walter, Sugg & Moore, 2001). Curfewees concede that it is irksome but preferable to prison, and their families mostly prefer it, although Smith (2001) noted increases of heightened domestic stress as a result. These kinds of research findings, together with the marginalizing of Napo as a voice in penal policy, and generational change in probation service personnel – an influx of staff who have not inherited the social work ethos of the past, and who are less technophobic – has effectively ended opposition to the development of EM. An ever-rising prison population, for both men and women, making England and Wales the highest prison user in Europe, has focused the penal reform organizations on what it might take to bring it down. Nacro, England's largest service-providing penal reform organization remains sceptical of EM, especially for young offenders, but accepts it if it is used – as it is in ISSP – in conjunction with rehabilitative programmes.

The acceptance of EM by organizations once hostile to it is best illustrated by the recommendations of the Committee on Women's Imprisonment (the Wedderburn Committee), set up by the Prison Reform Trust in 1999. The Committee's rationale was the marked increase in the numbers of women sentenced to prison for low-seriousness offences, significantly more of whom were primary carers of children than men, far from home, coupled with the demonstrable inadequacy of the regimes in many women's prisons. Its central recommendation was for a drastic reduction in imprisonment for women, made possible by much greater use of *new and existing* community penalties. Although its strongest commitment was to rehabilitative and reintegrative measures that met needs and empowered women, the Committee took for granted that EM could be a useful ingredient in community penalties, and accepted its potential for women:

The opportunities to divert women offenders from custody to punishment in the community have never been greater. The courts now have a range of penalties, supported by electronic tagging, that can restrict the liberty of the offender to a degree that was previously unattainable in a community setting. (Committee on Women's Imprisonment, 2000, para. 5:31) ...

The introduction of the electronic tag has been controversial, with some critics claiming that it violates the personal integrity of the offender. Undoubtedly it is a highly intrusive device but one that may in our view be justified if it facilitates the principle of parsimony in delivering punishment. (Ibid., para. 5:47)

This proposal gained active support from most other penal reform groups, from involved churches, and even from the most radical of women penal reformers in Britain.[8] Government support for Wedderburn was initially unforthcoming, although its eventual strategies for women offenders acknowledged the importance of non-custodial penalties. Nonetheless, two new women's prisons were also planned, to be run by the private sector, which hardly suggested an unalloyed commitment to reducing prison use for women.

The private companies who administer EM in Britain have a low public profile but the increasing scale of EM's use – and the involvement of two of the companies in private prisons – makes them potentially significant players in criminal justice politics. Chubb and Marconi, who were involved in the 1989 trials, have dropped out and services are currently provided on a three-region basis in England (the North; the Midlands, the East and London; and the South) by Securicor, Premier and Reliance respectively. Only Securicor – English-owned but with global interests in prison and EM provision[9] – has been involved from the outset; the others have been subject to shifting patterns of ownership. Premier was originally a prison-providing consortium organization half-owned by the American Wackenhut Corrections Corporation; it entered the EM field by buying the small indigenous locator-technology company, Geografix, which had piloted some of the curfew order experiments. Wackenhut was in turn taken over by Danish-based Group 4 Falke in May 2002, making it 'the world's largest security company' (Prison Privatisation Report International, 2002). Reliance, a British security company, took over from GSSC Europe (a subsidiary of an American company who had held the original contract in southern England) in October and gained the entire Scottish contract in January 2002. It is thus meaningful to speak of an international EM 'industry', although it has amorphous boundaries and deep roots in information and communications technology (ICT), connections to the defence and private security industries and the commercial-corrections complex. Next to nothing is publicly known about the internal operation, the social ambitions or the lobbying activities of the private organizations involved in EM and imprisonment, and they rarely enter public debate – indeed, they are contractually discouraged by the Home Office from doing so. One monitoring company manager told me that they wanted to be seen as 'a new player in criminal justice – not just some kind of security firm' (personal communication, March 16, 2002), which implies an ambition beyond being a mere service provider, beholden to the purposes of others.

EM, it must be remembered, is not just a technology – there is a significant element of human labour involved in its administration, and stories about the amount of data that EM systems can generate, which requires processing, appraisal and reaction *by people* (at least at present) are among the key cautionary tales attending EM's development (Baumer & Mendelsohn, 1995). All three monitoring companies employ large numbers of monitoring staff, either in their control rooms (collating, assessing and judging data) or as field staff (fitting and retrieving tags, checking violations, repairing equipment). Little is known about the background of the people being recruited, but they are not regarded as needing the full social work skills or sense of perspective that probation officers have traditionally possessed. Vocational training for such staff is being provided by the Custodial Care National Training Organisation, which sets standards and trains staff in prisons, immigration detention centres, secure accommodation for juveniles, military corrections and court escort services. It is possible that a new criminal justice occupation is being born within the monitoring companies, separate from youth justice and probation staff, which powerfully reinforces the idea that EM is a *parallel* rather than an *integrated* development in British criminal justice. New uses, already legislated, are envisaged for EM, and its future seems assured.

Paradoxically, the expansion of EM has occurred despite the wider media debate neither welcoming it as a tough and constructive solution to prison overcrowding, nor fearing it as a dehumanizing, Orwellian invasion of civil liberties (Nellis, 2003). Press coverage of EM in Britain has, with rare exception, questioned or even derided the idea that EM amounts to a serious punishment or an adequate constraint on offenders' behaviour. This was particularly true in February/March 2002, when the government's proposal to extend its use to young offenders on bail was severely criticized in the press, abetted strongly by police organizations who were sceptical of its potential (and, at that time, at odds with government on a variety of issues). Particularly paradoxically for the once hostile probation service, EM has been portrayed in the press as something *akin to* probation rather than a threat to it, yet another means of letting offenders avoid the only *real* punishment, imprisonment. Quite why this has happened is complex, but it partly reflects the increasingly acknowledged tension between managerial and technocratic controls (which EM exemplifies) and the more visceral, volatile and ostentatious harm to offenders which 'popular punitivism' seemingly demands.

Although at first sight EM can easily be characterized as a punishment because of the way it restricts liberty and regulates an offender's use of time – commonplace characteristics of punishment – it has been vulnerable to the criticism that there is something inherently lenient about allowing offenders to live in the assumed comfort of their own homes, perhaps with their families (exactly as other community penalties usually do). Offenders' accounts of the experience suggest that it is usually experienced as unpleasant, and particularly to a younger generation of people whose lifestyles are not home-centred, home confinement might understandably be psychologically painful.[10] As Bauman (2000) says (with prison in mind), immobilization is indeed a severe penalty in a world where self-realization requires mobility. But this idea can be pressed too far, for EM remains a 'responsibilized' punishment – though less so than probation – which does not immobilize quite as literally as imprisonment; nor is it the late-modern equivalent of a 'ball and chain', as some have claimed (Gibbs & King, 2002). The offender can if s/he *chooses*, remove or disregard the tag, and take, or seek to evade, the consequences. EM is thus better understood not as a form of immobilization, but more as a way of pinpointing and locating people.

Therein lies a further reason why it cannot unequivocally be portrayed as punishment, because locatability has become a relatively commonplace experience in late modernity – signified by pagers and mobile phones – an aspect of privacy that as citizens and consumers, we have traded out of necessity (employers and customers want to know where we are), convenience and security (to keep in touch with friends and family). The state-imposed locatability that is entailed by EM is obviously different from the self-chosen locatability of mobile phone users, but it is recognizably on the same continuum of experience, and made possible by the same ICT infrastructure, and is therefore a little less distinctive as a punishment, a little less 'other' than it might once have appeared.

ELECTRONIC MONITORING AND THE FUTURE OF COMMUNITY PENALTIES

The nature of community penalties is changing, but not just because of EM. There is an ever-wider array of them, whose precise purpose and implementation is specified in advance by government, by national standards and required programmes, rather than being left to the discretion of sentencers of probation and youth justice staff. Beyond a shared ethos of crime reduction and public protection, there is a sharper differentiation of purpose among such penalties, downplaying rehabilitation in some respects (the name of the community *service* order was changed to community *punishment* order to reflect this); emphasizing 'coercive rehabilitation' in respect of probation (now called a community rehabilitation order) and penalties focused on drug use; and sometimes emphasizing restorative justice (especially for young offenders). Despite being more demanding and controlling, community penalties are increasingly being used for lower-seriousness, low-risk offenders (traditional anxieties about net-widening are declining), and breach criteria are tighter, with imprisonment the most likely specified outcome of a return to court.

More subtly, there appears to be an emerging trend towards building elements of 'civic disqualification' into community penalties, e.g. removing benefit entitlements to ensure conformity with their requirements. Insofar as they remove entitlements to a mobility that a free citizen would take for granted, electronically monitored curfews (and exclusion orders, once on stream) can be regarded as disqualificatory penalties. Curfew orders have mostly been used with lower-risk offenders (who might nonetheless have been imprisoned), and unlike all other community penalties apart from hostels, they can exert a significant degree of control at night.

Moreover, there has been a corresponding weakening of key elements in more traditional community penalties, notably their humanistic, rounded concern with individual offenders, whose decline creates both an opening and a need for more surveillance-oriented practice. The rehabilitative ethic of the probation service nominally remains but is being eroded from within, mostly by managerialism. The emphasis is more on encouraging conformity to external requirements than on internal change and a meaningful 'responsibilization'. Managerialism (reduced professional discretion and personal influence, greater prescriptiveness, specified targets and performance indicators) normalizes surveillance of *both* staff and offenders (more monitoring and auditing) and simultaneously weakens the prime sources of resistance to it (effective control through relationships, personal bonds, trust). Within a managerial milieu, otherwise valuable cognitive behavioural programmes become unnecessarily coercive, and ideas about helping and supporting offenders are devalued. Consistent with these cultural changes, the Service has been given a surveillance role in respect of serious and high-risk offenders, particularly predatory sex offenders, requiring routine information-sharing with the police and creating what Nash calls the hybrid role of 'polibation officer'; as he observes, the 'service is now much more ready to discuss surveillance, control, risk management and reduction than previously' (1999, p. 367).

There are also institutional reasons for thinking that the probation service is an organization in decline, one whose continued existence as a separate organization cannot be taken for granted. One of the New Labour government's first acts (in 1997) was to suggest the idea of merging the prison and probation service into a single 'correctional agency'. Explicit resistance from both agencies, and from the judiciary and the magistracy, prevented this from happening when it was first mooted. Nonetheless, there are reasons for thinking that the organizational changes that took place in April 2001 represented a compromise position, and that a merger agenda is being pursued obliquely within the Home Office, although analysts remain uncertain about this (Cannings, 2002).

The desirability of a single correctional agency, in which traditional obstacles to communication and planning between prison and probation would allegedly be overcome, is evident in the Home Office's review of sentencing (Halliday, 2001). This is not stated explicitly, but the level of cooperation required to achieve some of the report's sentencing goals seems to point inexorably towards it. The keystone of the report is the idea of 'the seamless sentence', which combines custodial and community elements into a single entity, the latter part being understood not, as in the past, as low key 'aftercare' but as an integral element of the whole sentence. (The Detention and Training Order, introduced for young offenders in 1998, was a prototype of this.) The intention is that any rehabilitative work begun in prison will be continued in the resettlement phase more consistently and rigorously than previously, with the threat of recall for non-compliance. In addition, Halliday proposed a new set of 'intermediate sanctions' and a singe generic community penalty. The origins of the seamless sentence probably lie in despondent recognition that the long-sought Holy Grail of liberal penal policy – gaining public support for 'tough' community penalties – could never be won, even with EM as its mainstay. This development significantly undermines the logic that has traditionally legitimated the existence of *separate* prison and probation agencies: seamless sentences may require a seamless agency.

Many of Halliday's proposals were embodied in the White Paper *Justice for All* (Home Office, 2002). Electronic monitoring of some kind, not necessarily within current legal frameworks, was integral to its conception of the post-prison part of seamless sentences, and, indeed, to other sentencing proposals in the report. HDC was seen by Halliday as a prototype that had proved its worth, but:

> its capacity to support resettlement objectives is *underexploited*. A great deal can be done to make release planning and management of the prisoners' return to the community more effective, buttressing curfews, and electronic monitoring where necessary, with programmes to meet identifiable needs. (Halliday, 2001, 4.10, emphasis added)

Halliday characterized EM as a 'protective', controlling rather than a 'rehabilitative' measure and while seemingly allowing for the possibility of it being used as a stand-alone penalty, generally favoured sentences with multiple ingredients – punishment, rehabilitation and reparation. EM's contribution to intermittent penalties was explicitly linked to containment: 'some of the effects of intermittent custody could be achieved through intermittent containment in the community – by using attendance and residence requirements and curfews with electronic monitoring to impose a kind of "house arrest"' (Halliday, 2001, 0.15). The report took for granted the existence of electronic monitoring providers as a presence on the criminal justice scene, and proposed a new statutory duty on them, the police and the probation service to cooperate in the supervision of offenders in the community (ibid., 0.21).

TOWARDS DISPLACEMENT AND SUPERCESSION

The shift from a humanistic to a surveillant paradigm in work with offenders, however, has already begun, and, as Lyon (2001a) implies, there is more to this than technology. Underpinning surveillance technology generally is 'an idolatrous dream of omniperception, a desire to see and know (and preferably anticipate) everything, to penetrate all surfaces', combined with a belief that sooner or later this will be technically accomplished. 'This dream', he writes, 'lends a vital thrust to the constant upgrading and extension of surveillance' (ibid., p. 147). At heart this is a socio-political dream, a desire for a distinctive managerialist vision of social ordering, and it is this, rather than technology *per se*, that constitutes a threat to humanistic values.

Integral to this longing for omniperception and perfect, meticulous control is a Manichean sensibility – a composite mood of suspicion, fear and hatred – which sees threat and danger everywhere and encourages the development of a permanent watchfulness, tight controls and, as the ultimate backstop, tough punishments. Judged against this ideal of meticulous order the 'normal' vitality and unpredictability of human beings is interpreted to indicate their inherently unruly or intractably wicked nature – a chilling perception, which in turn galvanizes renewed attempts at exclusion or repression. Humanistic values premised on the idea that people are rarely wholly bad, that they are educable and have the capacity to change for the better, and that 'tough love' has something to offer – all of which traditionally informed probation and youth justice – are inevitably corroded by these developments.

The danger in administrative criminological debate is to regard EM *merely* as a discrete example of a new community penalty or a new form of post-release supervision. It is far better understood as one aspect of what Haggerty and Ericson (2000) call 'the surveillant assemblage' and seen in this light it can be perceived as consonant with three emergent and related trends in social ordering and social control, whose implications for existing forms of work with offenders have not, in the main, been recognized.

First, ICT has made possible degrees of control-at-a-distance and in real time that were hitherto impossible. Highly centralized organizations can gather and process information from the periphery of the spatial area in which they have jurisdiction, and issue complex instructions back with unparalleled speed; continuous, meticulous and just-in-time control (or at least oversight) is becoming an ideal of offender governance, which an intrinsically slower and more intermittent form of control (e.g. old-fashioned probation) cannot hope to emulate. The speeding-up of crime control processes – the acceleration of policy and legislative cycles, reducing delay in courts, fast-tracking of serious cases, administering instant fines (by police, not courts), and rapid police response to CCTV imagery – is evidence of shifting time horizons in criminal justice (and in governance generally); interest in the increasingly chimerical 'long term' is giving ground to a desire to exert control in the here and now. EM can do this more tangibly and definitively than probation.

Second, organizational decision-making increasingly relies on 'virtuality' – the computerized creation of digital personae from a variety of data streams (in the case of EM, risk profiles; curfew schedules; records of conversation with monitors) whose analysis may have fateful consequences for the offender concerned. EM is an *individuated*, precisely targeted intervention, but is not an *individualized* (i.e. personalized) response to offending whose efficacy depends on understanding and relating to a person (as probation once was); used on its own, EM generates data (e.g. the accumulation of precisely timed violations) on which breach judgments can be made without any empathic human understanding being factored in. In *any* computerized record, the simulated, digital personae may be a more tangible reality to monitors and decision makers than the actual human person whom they ostensibly signify: EM is simply an instance of this.

Third, EM exemplifies the growth of surveillance techniques targeted on the body (rather than the mind, through an appeal to reason, conscience or self-interest), obviating the need to make the effort of understanding. The tag, something physically attached to the body, is the crudest version of this; variants of tags that can measure alcohol intake, and certainly voice verification, take EM into the realm of biometric surveillance. Brian Bloomfield, a management theorist, sees the tagging of human bodies merely as one aspect of what he calls 'the generality of the concept of tagging', an already established and still evolving solution to problems of spatial and temporal coordination in complex, fast-paced societies. All that is entailed is the attachment of an identifier (e.g. a bar code, an encrypted password, a vehicle locator device, an electronic tag) to specified objects (or people) so that they can be tracked, traced and positioned 'in the right place at the right time'. This creates the possibility of 'authorised and non-authorised movements of subjects in time':

> We are witnessing a wholesale shift towards the instituting of a world where every object whose movement is potentially problematic (as regards, for example, matters of ownership, identity or organisation) may become subject to electronic sur-

veillance, a world where all such objects will have a form of electronic identity. (Bloomfield, 2001, p. 183)

Despite the demonstrable momentum behind each of the above developments, they are not guarantees that EM's route to dominance in the community penalty field – or its transformation of that field – will be smooth or without setbacks, or that its development will be beyond the vicissitudes of politics. There is no inexorable logic to them: as Sparks (2000b, p. 139) rightly says 'advances and retrenchments in penal technique', often contingently connected to emotive moments (dramatic crimes, prison riots, scandalous political ineptitude etc.), are unlikely to disappear from criminal justice. The 'popular punitive' mood (rooted in the pervasive insecurities of late modernity) will remain significant for the foreseeable future, and will presumably continue to disdain tagging as an adequate response to crime. Efforts to brand EM as 'suitably' punitive, or punitive 'enough' will doubtless also continue. The Halliday Review (2001, 2.35) of sentencing described EM as 'visibly punitive', but there are definite limits on the extent to which EM can be portrayed as such, especially when it is also used with the as yet unconvicted. Nonetheless, despite a severe press mauling over its February/March 2002 initiative to tag young bailees (a classic moment of 'popular punitive' rage) the Home Office has pressed on with it, apparently confident that it can show tagging to be *controlling enough*, if not punitive. What was equally clear from this episode was that the Home Office never publicly endorses the humanistic aspects of probation and youth justice with the same vigour as it endorses EM, presumably because it doubts if arguments premised on humanism possess the potency and credibility of technological arguments.

The managerialist ideal of technocentric, meticulous, here-and-now control-at-a-distance, nowadays inextricably meshed with ICT (Jones, 2000), supplies the higher logic that drives the expansion of EM. Since Peters first noted that 'many of the earlier humanitarian ideals [in criminal justice] have been lost in a drift towards business-like, centralised, bureaucratised and efficiency-oriented policies in which financial and quantitative considerations loom larger than the philosophy of resocialisation' (1986, p. 32), the concept of managerialism has been progressively refined. Scheerer, for example, astutely recognized that 'managerialism gives a boon to technical controls that display some kind of elective affinity to it' and saw just such an affinity between 'managerialism and electronic monitoring' (2000, p. 251). He also grasped that the element of perpetual, or at least periodic, surveillance that managerialism in general entails begins to reconfigure the entire field of community supervision and to alter both the mode and the scheduling of intervention in offenders' lives:

> it will become of paramount importance to collect knowledge and to be able to pinpoint persons and things – and it will become less imperative to catch every offender at the earliest possible time, since that could prevent the collection of further knowledge about his contacts, his plans and possible criminal organisations so police will want to accumulate knowledge more than to react to single offences. (Ibid.)

In making possible new forms of exclusionary or disqualificatory control (or perhaps reconfiguring old ones) EM arguably makes punishment less necessary as a particular, and traditional, end point of the prosecution process. It revitalizes the old community penalty ideal of 'conditional liberty', creating for the individual offender an ambience in which the physical signs of confinement are visibly absent, but in which their presence or absence in particular places (and, in future, their movements) is 'virtually' knowable to unseen others. Unlike earlier forms of conditional liberty, EM facilitates enhanced detectability, and by implication deterrence, via *'prima facie* evidence provided by the electronic system that a rule either has been followed or been violated' (Jones, 2000, p. 11).

The danger with the managerialist ideal of efficient, meticulous regulation is that, as Fionda notes, it 'has no natural limits' (2000, p. 127) – its animating vision gives it 'every incentive to evade limitations' – moral or otherwise – which impede the regulation of ever-more microscopic aspects of organizational (and communal) behaviour. Once this ideal – another way of expressing what Lyon calls the 'dream of omniperception' – is understood as informing the milieu in which EM is developing, it is clear that tagging in its present technical form is less of a worry than the underlying desires and ambitions that are shaping its development. The distant ideal is the micro-management of offenders' lives, and present practice, even when augmented by existing technology, patently falls short of this. It is merely a step in what is currently a politically desired direction, and a crude step at that. The ideal itself may never be properly achieved – few penal ideals have been – but strengthened on a 'so far, so good' basis, it inspires a continuing search for better ways of realizing itself; as Bloomfield notes, each successive generation of surveillance technology carries within it 'the germ of its own continual obsolescence' (2001, p. 191).

No assumption, however, is being made here that this transition signals the emergence of a strengthened state with an *actually* increased capacity to control its subject-citizens. As both Garland (1996) and Scheerer (2000) have argued, state sovereignty is declining and, although the means may be different from what we have now, future crime control may be tentative, ramshackle and haphazard in its effects rather than streamlined and proficient. British society will probably not be safer or more secure, violent crime may well increase (and/or change its forms), and prison may well be used more. All I am suggesting is the likelihood of an institutional reconfiguration of the agencies involved in community supervision (whether instead of, or after, prison) that leaves the providers and managers of EM in a stronger position vis-à-vis traditional agencies. Present managerial trends point towards the displacement of community penalties (or the community components in seamless sentences) in which humanistic elements are dominant, by community penalties in which surveillant elements are dominant. Thus, whereas in the past there were probation orders to which additional requirements (for treatment or control purposes) were added, the future may see community punishment orders (with EM taken for granted), to which a probation or supervision requirement may or may not be added, depending on whether or not sentencers want help, support or offence confrontation offered to an offender as well. Signs of this instability and pointers towards the future positioning of EM can arguably be inferred from press coverage, in which tagging gains in credibility not as something that can supplement probation service or youth justice programmes, but as something more akin to a suspended sentence, which fosters prudent behaviour in offenders primarily because it is backed up by prison:

> tagging will only work when these hardened youths will know that the penalty for breaking the curfew is jail. (*Daily Express*, February 27, 2002)

By early 2002 it was clear that the government was sufficiently confident about EM to permit and live with the kind of failures (and consequent criticism) that expanding HDC and extending the scheme to juveniles will inevitably entail. Failure, of course, never matters in criminal justice policy in quite the way that rationally inclined analysts, seduced by the prevailing discourse of evidence-led policy and practice, believe. For all the talk about 'cracking crime' modern politicians have long learned to live with high levels of failure: there are never real solutions, only eye-catching (and vote-catching) initiatives. Sometimes there are paradigm shifts, like the shift from humanistic to surveillant practice that is arguably occurring now, but more usually, the search for improvement occurs within rather narrow policy parameters. Once the surveillant paradigm becomes established, the failure of one sort of electronic surveillance will thus lead to a search for new sorts of electronic surveillance – abetted by the rapid obsolescence of each generation of technology, and the sophisticated marketing of the new – rather than to a reversion to more humanistic forms of control like old-style probation. It will probably follow the pattern that probation itself has followed since the mid-twentieth century: as one sort of probation 'failed', new, tougher,[11] *more intensive* types were sought, until probation itself had become a species of control and surveillance, *but of an inherently limited kind that cannot compete with 'the real thing'.*

CONCLUSION

Feeley and Simon's observation that 'new formations rarely grow on ground totally cleared of the past' (1994, p. 178) is an apt description of the situation in which the providers and supporters of EM find themselves. EM constitutes a new form of community (non-prison) control growing – both technologically and organizationally – in the interstices and on the margins of the old forms. The old is not yet vanquished – and indeed, need not be vanquished – but despite appearances to the contrary, it is losing vigour and purpose. Present forms of EM ('tagging') are still new, still evolving, barely beyond the prototype stage – and could eventually be developed, both technically and discursively, as a more draconian form of control (longer time periods, tight breach criteria, guaranteed imprisonment for breach) even if, short of pain-inflicting potential,[12] it always falls short of being 'proper' punishment. The supplementary phase – assisting in the achievement of humanistic goals – is passing: the dream of omniperception beckons beyond it, and humanistic ideals are in any case fading from contemporary public life. A threshold of acceptability has already been crossed, and tagging is now sufficiently embedded in British criminal justice that, for all its manifest limitations, any political attempt to cease using it, and to revert back to purely humanistic forms of control, would inevitably be portrayed in the media as retrograde and soft on crime.

The electronic monitoring of offenders, in some shape or form, will also gain in cultural and political credibility (and prestige), at traditional probation's expense, as other forms of surveillance are normalized within criminal justice (and society generally), and will on occasion, if not always as a rule, be meshed with them. In the overall 'surveillant assemblage' (Haggerty & Ericson, 2000) EM may not be the most prominent or important element in a supervision package, but its inclusion is always likely to be considered. In its inaugural column on technology-for-corrections (itself a sign of the times),[13] the American journal *Federal Probation* offered this multiple-tool scenario:

> As those under criminal justice supervision have fewer privacy protections than ordinary citizens, systems that track many aspects of their lives such as their whereabouts, access to computers, or financial records, may become commonplace. One can imagine a convicted Internet seller of child pornography whose movements are being monitored via satellite, his computer files tracked via biometric devices, and financial database records searched periodically to see if he has illegal sources of income. (Greek, 2000, p. 61)

Such scenarios cannot be dismissed as groundless, in Britain or in any Western country, and, one might ask, where will the probation service figure in them, if at all? The normalization of locatability, the ascendancy of managerialism, the growing power of the private sector, the possibility of mass customization and the astonishing, extraordinary advances in surveillance practice over the past decade should make us very wary of denying EM's *potential* to follow the general trajectory outlined in this chapter. Primo Levi said of the concentration camps that they were 'the product of a conception of the world carried rigorously to its logical conclusion; so long as the conception subsists, the conclusion remains to threaten us' (1979, p. 15). There are new anti-humanist conceptions now – the dystopian dream of omniperception is one – and a rising class of techni- cians and managerialists committed to their realization, and whose logical conclusions are scarcely less alarming. There is undeniably momentum behind managerialism, a correspond- ingly forceful logic to surveillance and a waning of humanistic ideals in criminal justice, all of which favour the continuing expansion of EM at the expense of more traditional community penalties. Add to this the existence of a globally powerful private sector with a commercial incentive to see EM develop further, and the scene is set for a very significant transformation in the way in which offenders are supervised before, after and – all too infrequently – instead of prison.

NOTES

1. Lynsey Bass of the Youth Justice Board, Chris Stanley and Scott Cadman of Nacro, Jackie Knox of the Scottish Executive, and James Toon (current Head of the Home Office's Electronic Monitoring Unit) helped with the preparation of this chapter. Several conversations with Bob Lilly in the summer of 2001 and the spring of 2002 lie in the background. In informal conversation, rather than in a formal research interview, two monitoring company personnel supplied me with telling quotations used in the chapter – one of which forms the title – but I do not feel at liberty to identify them.

2. Although EM developed first in the US in the context of the 'interme- diate sanctions' movement it was not called 'tagging' there. It was originally linked by name to 'house arrest' (a penalty available in some US states prior to the advent of EM), and later 'home confinement', 'home detention' and 'home incarceration' to give it the requisite con- trolling and punitive connotations. In Britain, Tom Stacey named it

'tagging' in the letter to *The Times* in 1982 that publicly launched his campaign to establish EM here (Stacey, 1993) – being primarily interested in tracking offenders' movements, he did not use the term 'curfew'. Quite apart from the commonplace American use of the word 'tag' to mean, among other things, a graffiti-artist's signature, Annesley Schmidt, a key figure in EM's development in America, did not apparently like the term 'tagging', possibly because it was thought a demeaning thing to do to human beings, given the way 'ear-tags' were used on animals. According to Bob Lilly (e-mail February 28, 2003) 'Behavioural Interventions Inc's original Goss-Link was a spin off from the technology used to put "ear tags" on cattle in massive stinking feedlots in order to control feedings', and rather understandably, that was not an image which the promoters of EM believed would best serve their cause. Insofar as names can affect images, which in turn affect how a penalty can be positioned in public, professional and political debate, the technology-cum-purpose of 'EM' has always been difficult to characterize definitively – a degree of discursive imprecision invariably lingers. Mark Renzema (e-mail March 28, 2002) rightly points out that even the terms 'electronic monitoring' and 'electronic surveillance' connote a range of privacy-invading technologies very different from what England calls 'tagging'. His favoured term for the technology would be 'automatic curfew checking' – but he concedes that in America 'most illusions of punitiveness and safety would vanish' if this were ever adopted. Curfew (originally meaning 'night-time confinement') does seemingly have punitive (as well as 'emergency powers') connotations in England: it has existed as a bail condition for many years, as a sentence since 1982 – which was largely thought unenforceable by human means (Tildesley & Bullock, 1983), and was hardly used until EM augmented it. Some analysts and commentators on EM have used the term 'electronic leash' (Marx, 1988; Zonderman, 1990) to metaphorically convey its function, and although this has not caught on in legal or policy circles, EM is known, uniquely, in the state of Michigan, as 'tethering', an ostensibly equine metaphor whose origins Renzema (e-mail March 28, 2002) is unaware of.

3. One of the few 'liberal' things that Michael Howard did, in the face of incontrovertible evidence that too many fine defaulters were being indiscriminately imprisoned, was to vary the penalty that courts could impose for this, by permitting community service, electronically monitored curfew and driving disqualification as well as prison. In the pilots, community service was by far the most popular measure among magistrates, who, according to the Home Office researchers, said they preferred it

> because it is more positive than tagging or driving disqualification. The offender is seen to be putting something back into society. The perceived expense of tagging and the misconception that curfews should only be used when they could have a preventive effect could be limiting take up of this measure. (Elliot, Airs & Webb, 1999, p. 3)

4. Tony Blair, the architect of New Labour thinking, whilst Opposition Home Affairs Spokesman, seemingly made no specific comment on EM. His predecessor in this post, Roy Hattersley, an emphatically Old Labour politician, was hostile to it. In the course of debates on the curfew order in the Criminal Justice Bill 1990 he said:

> Electronic tagging would be a farce if it was ever implemented in this country. We have read encouraging reports in serious newspapers that, while the Government feel that they must save face by going ahead with the clauses, they have no intention of implementing the proposal. (Parl Debates 181 (6th ser.) col. 160, November 20, 1990 (quoted in Windelsham, 2001, p. 291))

This interpretation of events at the start of the 1990s, implying that the then Conservative Home Office faltered in its commitment to EM, can, however, be contested. James Toon (current Head of the Home Office's Electronic Monitoring Unit) assures me (personal communication, June 13, 2002) that in the early 1990s ministers were *very keen* to continue using EM, but because of a genuine mistake in the drafting of the CJA 1991, *which permitted national provision of EM but not experimental piloting*, they were simply unable – but far from unwilling – to proceed as they wished. A crowded legislative timetable meant that there was no opportunity to rectify this mistake until the Criminal Justice and Public Order Act 1994.

5. Two hundred of the original 14,000 released on HDC reoffended – an exceptionally small proportion – but this was amplified out of all proportion by the Conservative Opposition in what proved to be a forlorn attempt to make the New Labour government seem irresponsible in releasing prisoners early. Aghast that people of his own political persuasion should disparage HDC, Tom Stacey wrote to the *Daily Telegraph* (March 30, 2000) to protest that the Opposition was 'rubbishing an essentially Conservative initiative'. The reoffences included two rapes, but by men whose risk assessment could probably not have anticipated this because they had no previous record of such offences. Nonetheless, the 'myth' of HDC's failure is unlikely to die just yet. Police officer Norman Brennan, spokesperson for the Victims of Crime Trust, indicated on a BBC news programme (March 2002) the form that criticism may take: 'The victims of the rapes and other crimes should take legal action against the government. They would not have been attacked if the men had been in prison ... The system is crazy, we are letting convicted criminals out to cause mayhem.'

6. It is possible that the introduction of tagging for juveniles followed open acknowledgement by the Home Office that the local child curfew schemes (area-based prohibitions, not electronically monitored) it had introduced in the Crime and Order Act 1998 had been unsuccessful. The Act empowered local authorities to apply for a blanket geographical curfew on under-10s, prohibiting them from being outside between 9 p.m. and 7 a.m. No local authority applied for such a ban. The scheme was nonetheless extended in August 2001 to include under-15s, and the police were also given the power to apply for one. By the end of 2001,

despite oft-expressed police concern about rising juvenile crime, none of these collective curfews had been applied for. Napo, which had long ridiculed the imposition of 'a national bedtime' reaffirmed its opposition to the very principle of these schemes (*Napo News* 136. February 2002, p. 3).

7. Satellite tracking has already been undertaken experimentally in the US (particularly in Florida) and is likely to become more widespread (Renzema, 1998a; 1998b; 1999; 2000; Johnston & Grinter, 1998). It is likely to be used in Britain, although there are practical tracking technologies using radio cells that are not dependent on satellites; one such is already in use in Sydney, Australia. Satellite tracking may not happen until Britain – and Europe more generally – has its own system of satellites. This, at least, is in hand. The European Union and the European Space Agency plans to establish Galileo, a 30-satellite global surveillance system, in 2008 to rival America's GPS system and Russia's Glonass system. Both of these are essentially military systems, in which civil organizations rent use. European countries fear that America, which neither guarantees signal cover nor accepts financial liability for breakdowns, may turn off its satellites during war or political disputes, and want a system under its own control. Recent car tracking and road pricing proposals in Britain depend on the development of Galileo, but it will have a wide variety of military, commercial and civil purposes (Walters, 2002). Researchers propose that by 2010 all cars should be fitted with dashboard signalling devices, allowing all their movements to be satellite-tracked by a computer at GCHQ, Cheltenham. The civil liberty implications of this proposal are immense, but even a *Guardian* (liberal newspaper) editorial (February 25, 2002) accepted that Britain's traffic congestion problem is so serious that even 'satellite tracking needs an open debate'.

8. Chris Tchaikovsky (1944–2002) was an ex-offender who founded Women In Prison, an abolitionist group that nonetheless evolved into small-scale service provision in HMP Holloway, London. Prison abolitionists, perhaps more so than liberal reformers, cannot afford to be too hasty in condemning EM if it is properly used to reduce prison use; its potential for net-widening does remain a problem. Tchaikovsky extolled the potential of EM for women offenders in the final plenary session of the 'Bad Girls? or Bad Times?' conference organized by Catholic Action for Social Care (CASC) in Leeds, November 25, 2000.

9. Securicor is a British firm founded (as Night Watch Services) in 1935 by a barrister, an aristocrat and a merchant banker to guard the homes of London's wealthy (Draper, 1971; Underwood, 1997). It steadily expanded into all areas of security provision, becoming prominent in Britain for cash transit in secure vehicles. Stacey (1995b) regards its Datatrack system, for monitoring the movement of these vehicles, as a prototype and precursor of tracking tagging; it was also the co-originator (with British Telecom) of Cellnet, Britain's first radio cell network. It now has a significant international presence, delivering EM in France and Australia, and in the US at state and local level. It claims to be the world leader in electronic monitoring services, having won a $30m contract with the Administrative Office of the United States Courts to

provide EM over five years at Federal level in all 50 states, plus Guam and Puerto Rico in 2002. It also runs private prisons around the world; its Dutch subsidiary has won the first private-sector detention contract (for drug-related offenders) in the Netherlands (www.securicor.com March 2002).

10. Insofar as the tag (or the transmitting equipment installed in offenders' homes) may be seen by others, it may be stigmatizing. Tom Stacey acknowledged that tagging may involve a useful element of disgrace. A letter to *The Times* in early 2002, seeking to offset the possibility of young male offenders regarding the wearing of a tag as a trophy, suggested that the tag 'should be pink, with pictures of Thomas the Tank Engine or Barbie displayed rather than plain grey. Youngsters would be mortified at the prospect of being made to look a fool, and might even think twice before offending again.' There are in fact serious issues here – there have been instances of tagged offenders being assaulted in the mistaken belief that they were sex offenders.

11. From at least the mid-twentieth century American science fiction writers have entertained the idea of monitoring citizens' or offenders' movements with tracking and tracing devices, which inflict psychic or physical – sometimes lethal – pain if the citizen/offender does not conform or strays into prohibited zones. In dystopian literature the possibility of pinpointing and locatability has generally been regarded as the epitome of totalitarian power. It is perhaps ironic that, culturally, the actual precursors of contemporary EM were all American (rather than Russian or Eastern European), and that a Spiderman comic (in which the villain tagged the hero) played a part in the imaginative breakthrough that led to EM (Fox, 1987). Science fiction stories that refer to 'tagging' peripherally or centrally are legion, with many permutations. A.E. van Vogt envisaged a future police state in which 'the electronic instrument "printed" on [a person's] right arm could be activated by any [police station], which would start a burning sensation of gradually increasing intensity' (1963, p. 42). Piers Anthony and Robert Margroff (1968) made a surgically attached, thought-monitoring, pain-inflicting 'ring' the centrepiece of a (very poor quality) futuristic crime thriller, which was nonetheless republished (1986) after EM had become a reality in the US. More speculatively, but in the same imaginative vein, R.C. Fitzpatrick (1967) envisaged future urban police stations being equipped with a kind of emotional radar (the deAngelis Board), sensitive to citizens' moods and able to pinpoint angry individuals who may erupt into violence, who are then pre-emptively arrested. (See Nellis (2003) on imaginary forms of electronic monitoring.)

12. The idea that tags could give electric shocks is not at all implausible. Surgical engineers, specifically Medtronic of Minneapolis, have already developed an 'implantable cardioverter defibrilator' (ICD), which monitors the timing of heartbeats and gives electric shocks of varying strengths to forestall impending heart attacks. The ICDs can be made to beep, to give advance warning of the coming shock. Some patients already have them fitted, including Vice-President Dick Cheney (Gallagher, 2001).

13. The application of technology to criminal justice is becoming an area of specialist expertise and is beginning to receive academic attention in Britain (Mair, 2001). There is as yet no equivalent in Britain of the US's Annual Innovative Technologies for Community Corrections Conference, the third of which took place in San Diego in 2002, but given the process of 'policy transfer', which is already of significance in the EM field (Nellis, 2000), it may only be a matter of time.

6
Information Warfare, Surveillance and Human Rights

Frank Webster

When most of us first think about surveillance a range of associations come to mind: the secret policeman tracking suspects, the accumulation of files on unpatriotic groups, the recording of attendance at meetings of subversives ... Today, of course, we would also insert the high-level technologies that accompany and assist in these sorts of activities, so we might add the image of the spook attaching a bugging device to someone's telephone, night-sights fixed to various sorts of binoculars, even geostationary satellites tracing car journeys of specified targets. One might account for such imaginings as overexposure to Ian Fleming and Frederick Forsyth, but I do think the imagery and associations contain a kernel of truth. The leading edge of surveillance is, indeed, that conducted by the state in pursuit of its security concerns. Much surveillance is about watching the enemy – within and without, potential and real. By the same token, surveillance is crucially about defence and its threatened accompaniment, war. Certainly it is in the realms of war/defence that the most sophisticated technologies of surveillance are found – in AWACS aircraft, in the global telecommunications eavesdropping network Echelon, in airborne drones packed with electronic devices capable of monitoring images thousands of feet below, analysing data and delivering weapons to targets with minimal human intervention.

From this it is an easy extension to argue that to understand surveillance it is essential to focus on the state, on its security requirements, and thereby on the imperatives of defence. In terms of this logic surveillance comes to be regarded as something found on the fringes of society, certainly not belonging to the mainstream, even if civil libertarians worry about intrusions on privacy of citizens. Up to a point I agree with this reasoning, but I would want to urge consideration of something that in my view gets too little attention from those interested in surveillance, and something that is a part of each of our everyday lives – the media. The media (and here I use a catholic definition of the term to encompass newspapers, television, radio, as well as newer information and communications technologies that support the Internet) are crucially about observation and analysis of people, places and events – all essentially surveillance activities. To be sure, media transmit as well as gather information, but too rarely are they included in considerations of surveillance, though they are intimately concerned with the practices of gathering and examining information. Commentary on surveillance tends to stick to the usual suspects of the military and security agencies, which are – unlike media – on the periphery of everyday life nowadays. In this chapter I want to argue that regarding the media as surveillance organizations can be illuminating. Indeed, I want to suggest that media have become a critical dimension of contemporary surveillance and, moreover, that attention to it can alert us to important changes in the character of warfare.

With respect to the media being engaged in surveillance, I am not referring here to the door-stepping of celebrities or of those unfortunate enough to be hit by exceptional and unexpected – and thereby newsworthy – events. What I want to do is relate media surveillance more directly to contemporary warfare, to suggest that media may now play an important role in both its commencement and conduct. Further, I do not want to deny that media can be little more than an extension of the surveillance activities of the state – that newspapers can seek out internal enemies ('fifth columnists'), and that they can readily become a *de facto* extension of the military endeavour by offering unqualified support to 'our boys'. However, in different circumstances – and I shall argue that some important circumstances have developed which do make things different nowadays – media can take on a very different role in warfare, one in which what they report, and how they report, may even alter the course of military action.

GLOBALIZATION

At the core of my argument should be placed the development of globalization, which exerts such significant pressure on the nation state system. There is a good deal of controversy as regards the degree to which globalization has extended and even how novel it is, but I think most commentators would concede that there has been an appreciable extension of the interpenetration, integration and interdependence of the world over recent decades. There can be no doubt that globalization has encouraged 'time-space compression' (Held et al., 1999), so much so that around the world times are coordinated, and the movement of goods and people is a great deal easier because of things such as airline travel, and this movement is almost immediate when it comes to informational matters (one thinks of real-time trading in stocks and shares, e-mail exchanges, and satellite television broadcasts). Globalization was accelerated by the collapse of Communism and the neo-liberal hegemony that has been unleashed, but also important has been the spread of an ICT (information and communications technology) infrastructure, which has facilitated the tendential spread of activities taking place on a planetary scale in real time (Castells, 1996–98).

GLOBALIZATION OF MEDIA

Most discussion and debate about globalization revolve around its economic and financial dimensions. However, when we conceive of globalization what should also be kept in mind is media. This has accompanied and expressed globalization with a vengeance, so much so that we may speak now of a common symbolic environment enveloping the world – Hollywood movies, soccer stars and their teams, soap operas such as *I Love Lucy* and westerns like *Bonanza*, and CNN and BBC news programmes (Tomlinson, 1999).

In making this bald statement I am conscious of a need to qualify: to observe that much of this reflects Western power structures, the dominance of the American star system, and that it is underpinned by technologies owned by concentrated economic interests (Schiller, 1981; 2000). It is beyond doubt that, while media now straddle the globe and content moves across borders with immediacy, the flows are heavily unidirectional – from the western and northern metropolitan centres to peripheral locations. Nevertheless, it must also be conceded, I think, that the globalization and growth of media has been an extraordinarily complex affair such that any generalizations about it oversimplify. In this light I would forward a number of propositions. First, the media explosion of recent decades has led to there being staggering amounts of information available today – anywhere, any time we have 24-hour news services, entertainment, radio talk shows and so on. This is inflected, to be sure, but there is such a quantity of information, in so many different outlets, coming with such velocity and with such turnover that, in a real sense, it is beyond control. That is, while we may agree that the media offer predominantly Western ways of seeing, there are many instances of countervailing messages being put out, sent in and received. In sum, whatever its overall limits, from today's media audiences can glean information about phenomena that is often counter to what one might presume is a 'Western interest' and, in turn, metropolitan viewers and listeners get access to information about events and issues, places and people, of which they are otherwise ignorant. All this, and we have not even mentioned the 'active audience' principle by which the dispositions of receivers are such to look out for information, and to filter what they receive, in ways that suit their interests and outlooks.

If there are elements of the media today that, because of their ubiquity and accessibility, are beyond the control of at least narrowly conceived state interests, there are two other features in particular that should be highlighted with regard to our concern for warfare. The first is that media are drawn, almost irresistibly, to cover warfare for several reasons. One is the obvious appeal of newsmakers towards the drama of conflict. It is truistic – but nonetheless important – to observe that the chances of getting noticed by the news are enhanced by sensational events, by high drama, by issues that have an urgent appeal (Chibnall, 1977). In these terms conflict situations are likely to achieve attention from the media, and war situations are the most likely of all conflict to get extensive coverage. The enormously high stakes, the life and death character of war, ensures that it is a priority for news media. To be sure, this does not mean that war is in itself sufficient to gain media attention – there are clearly other factors involved such as the scale and intensity of the conflict, its location, where the participants come from, as well as its strategic implications: so no one would suggest that war *per se* gets covered. Nor is one ignorant of media fatigue with regard to news coverage, such that wars which continue over time receive less coverage as the news from that source becomes 'old', though killing and destruction may persist. But the imperative of warfare being newsworthy remains and increases the likelihood of it receiving attention.

A second feature of media and warfare is the combination – one might even say tension – of the ethics of journalism and what one may describe as their cultivated cynicism towards sources of information as regards the conflicts they cover. It may be dangerous to raise the issue of professional ethics as regards journalists, since we are all familiar – at the least since Evelyn Waugh's *Scoop* (1938) – with the image of the 'hack' who rests comfortably in the international hotel, content to file his stories from official briefings; and the cynicism of journalists themselves, which does much to inform their reportage in war, can quickly deflate appeals to ethical behaviour (cf. Gall, 1994). Nevertheless, it remains the case that amongst the most revered journalists covering war – one might say the role models for aspirant journalists – are those with reputations for seeking 'truth', however much that might displease powerful interests.[1] One thinks here, for instance, of the late James Cameron's and Bert Hardy's reportage of ill-treatment of prisoners from Korea in the 1950s, Seymour Hersh's exposure of the Mai Lai massacre in Vietnam in the late 1960s, of William Shawcross's dispatches from Chile pointing the finger at US involvement following the Pinochet coup in 1973, of John Pilger's accounts of Cambodian atrocities in the early 1980s, of Robert Fisk's 30-year history of filing reports from Northern Ireland, Lebanon and Afghanistan, of Maggie O'Kane from the Balkans, of Suzanne Goldenberg's fearless accounts of the recent situation in Israel for the *Guardian* newspaper ... Phillip Knightley (2000) wrote a fine book on war reporting during the 1970s, which he titled 'the first casualty', and it is often so that truth is blurred in the fog of war; but Knightley himself, and many other war journalists, testify to an ethic of resistance to manipulation of news in warfare. This is not to say that this does not happen, but it is to stress that there is an ethic imbued into at least the better journalists that their mission is to 'tell it like it is', no matter how difficult that may be and no matter how unpopular this may make one with the powers that be. There may be something here of a heroic ideal[2] that cannot easily be matched in practice, but one need only recall that many journalists lose their lives in reporting from war situations[3] to realize that there is something of an ethical calling in the enterprise.

The cynicism must come from several sources, not least the experiences of the reporters in conflict situations, where they are likely to receive sharply conflicting accounts of events. However, a particular cause is surely the efforts of combatants to 'perception manage'. I shall say more about this later, but for now simply state that, notably since the Vietnam War and the defeat there of the United States, the notion that it was an uncontrolled media that led to American withdrawal gained ground amongst powerful figures in political and especially military circles. Beginning with Robert Elegant's (1981) bitter *Encounter* article, 'How to Lose a War', the conviction that media were important to war but not to be trusted, informed military and political 'planning for war'. With regard to the UK's activities in Northern Ireland (Curtis, 1984) and ever since the Falklands War in 1982, there has been a marked preparedness to 'handle' journalists, with 'minders' allocated, military spokespeople carefully groomed, and 'unfriendly' reporters held at bay. So self-conscious and developed is this process of 'perception management' that it is easy to believe that the outcome in terms of media coverage is entirely antiseptic – a one-way flood of items gathered away from the battlefield, at locations chosen by the military, and from handouts issued by the Ministry of Defence's PR staff. In certain circumstances, this may indeed be the case – coverage from the Falklands, far away in the South Atlantic, accessible only by military transport, and with the media reliant on military technologies to get their messages through is one such example (Morrison & Tumber, 1988). Against this, however, I would suggest that what the efforts to manage war coverage by those who wage it have done for journalists is bolster the scepticism of reporters. This does not mean that the military are neither able to constrain the media nor that they are unsuccessful in their attempts to convince the media to support the war effort. But I do think that it makes a cynical profession more cynical still when it notes the attempts of the military and official spokespeople to ensure that the media are 'on side'. In turn, this surely bolsters journalists' disposition to treat *all* sources sceptically, an important factor in what and how they report from the war zone. When one adds to this the fact that journalists nowadays converge on trouble spots from around the globe (though clearly in concentrations from more affluent regions), then one appreciates how difficult control becomes – it may just be possible for British military forces in Northern Ireland to appeal to the shared nationality of some reporters to self-censor their stories, but just what strength has this when applied to a journalist from Australia or Sweden? There were an estimated 2000 journalists in the Kosova region during 1999, and well in excess of 4000 in Iraq during the spring of 2003; it is simply too complex a situation and they are too variegated a bunch of people to be straightforwardly controlled.

Together these factors – pervasive media availability, the attraction of news agencies to war situations, professional ethics amongst journalists, and their entrenched scepticism – mean, I believe, that, however urgent and sustained the efforts of combatants to control and contain coverage, there will always be 'seepage' in what gets out. Bluntly, what gets covered and how it gets covered is subject to negotiation.

GLOBALIZATION AND THE
UNDERMINING OF THE NATION STATE

One needs to factor into the foregoing the important influence of globalization on the nation state. No one should think that the nation state is set to disappear in the recent future. The world's major nations remain intact – for example, China, India, the United States and the major European countries. Nevetheless, globalization does mean that nation states are increasingly 'porous' in just about every respect, from economic affairs to migrations of people. At the level of the symbolic, globalization means that nations are markedly less self-contained and exclusive than before, less able to contain the information people within receive and give out. On one level, this is a matter of technological change – cable and satellite television, and computer communications facilities, mean that it is increasingly difficult for nations to restrict what their inhabitants watch and send because technologies thwart attempts to do so. At another level, however, there is a worldwide decline of deference, an increased unwillingness to know one's place and not question what one's leaders do, which stimulates the development of information that is challenging and even critical. An important dimension of this tendency, to which I return below, is the global development of democracy and the human rights that accompany it. For now, however, I may illustrate this trend with two instances. One, the response to the attempted military coup in Russia during the summer of 1991. Here important sections of the military had announced a takeover and moved to strengthen their control, yet within a period of minutes Boris Yeltsin (who was undoubtedly courageous) was on television, mounted on a tank in front of the Kremlin, announcing his resistance, and e-mails were flying around the world decrying the military intervention. The planners of the coup had hoped to control the media, but lightweight cameras and modern computer communications foiled their intended surprise. Two, one is astonished to learn from his biographer (Horne, 1988; 1989) that the British Prime Minister from 1957 to 1963 (and Minister for Defence, Foreign Secretary and Chancellor of the Exchequer in the preceding three years), Harold Macmillan, held the highest offices while his wife continued an open and long-running affair (it lasted 40 years!) with a leading fellow Conservative, Robert Boothby, which resulted in one of Macmillan's putative children, Sarah, being fathered by Boothby. This, and the attendant misery, loneliness and stress (Macmillan suffered a massive nervous breakdown) was apparently known about in media circles at the time, but nothing was printed because it might 'damage the national interest'. It is unthinkable that such a sensational story would not today receive widespread notice, if not from domestic media pleading that effective government was jeopardized by such anguished relations (and tabloids driven to its salacious sides), then surely by a less inhibited foreign outlet.

One might add to this some observations on globalization's effect on economic matters, which are of enormous consequence. It was after the collapse of Communism around 1989 that globalization, if well in place, accelerated, on the back of a neo-liberal ascendancy. This brought with it a tendency towards the world being regarded as the core economic unit – whether in terms of dealing in foreign exchanges and investment, organizing production, or marketing products and services. This process is far from complete, of course, but as a tendential development it does announce the declining significance of territorial boundaries between nations.

An effect of globalization is stimulation of what Anthony Giddens has termed 'states without enemies' (Giddens, 1994, p. 235). The reasoning goes that, if there is large-scale crossover of ownership of capital, real-time movement, decision-making across borders, high levels of business and tourist migration, and increasing open markets and heightened trade around the globe, then there is a declining propensity for nations to go to war with one another over territory. As we shall see below, for the last several centuries war has been primarily about precisely this – land and the resources that accompanied its seizure by one side or the other. If it is the case that territory is no longer of such compelling importance in today's world, then logically it follows that states are less likely to have enemies with whom they may fight.

One might suppose that this heralds an era of world peace, but there are more negative effects of globalization, which stoke conflict. There is a toxic mix of increased inequalities on a global scale, with the poorest getting poorer,[4] frenetic change induced by heightened competition, marketization and technological innovation, and the spread of cosmopolitanism amongst those who participate in the world economy. The advantaged, those with access to capital and possessed of high-level education, may thrive in this world of flexibility, movement and restlessness, but the excluded and marginal find it deeply disconcerting and threatening. The globalization which demands of people that they change their ways as a matter of routine, that they abandon their cultures and take on more cosmopolitan forms, and that they be willing to adapt to market ways of life, may be met by those least well situated to gain with hostility and apprehension. In the view of several important commentators this is fertile ground for the strengthening of *fundamentalisms* of various sorts. Fundamentalism is an expression of certainty in an uncertain world – it is an insistence that some things are not subject to change or challenge, that there are some absolutes of morality, behaviour and belief (cf. Bauman, 1997). It may take many forms,[5] from born-again religion to neo-fascism, from an escape into asceticism to embrace of deep ecology – and it may also find outlets in militant zealotry, which can feed into terrorist organization and action.

In these circumstances we may experience the emergence of what Giddens (1994) terms 'enemies without states', where fundamentalists resist the 'Great Satan' of globalized and secular capitalism in the name of an absolutist creed that disregards national borders. This is the milieu in which al-Qaeda and the Osama bin Laden network is situated.[6] This reveals an enemy of globalization of which, after September 11, 2001, we are all well aware. However, it is a new sort of enemy, which poses serious problems for the state's conduct of war, which, traditionally, has been conducted against other nations in the name of defence of one's own country.

To summarize: I have argued that we might usefully see the media as forms of surveillance in so far as they are intimately engaged with monitoring, observing, analysing and assessing issues and events. I have suggested that globalization has made media pervasive and difficult to control effectively by the nation state, even in circumstances of extreme conflict such as warfare to which media are drawn. Finally, I have observed that a globalized world is increasingly one in which we have 'states without enemies' alongside the emergence of 'enemies without states'. This poses serious challenges to traditional reasons for and conduct of war, which have been concerned, by and large, with conflicts between nation states over territory (cf. Bobbitt, 2002).

This is a context in which profound questions are posed for media regarded as an agency of surveillance. If the context is one in which the media are more extensive and beyond control by the nation, while national boundaries and reasons for conducting war (and harnessing the media to that end) are diminishing, then what is the motivation for reporting disputes, what characteristics might this surveillance exhibit, and what might be its consequences? I think we may gain a better understanding of this by drawing a distinction – which itself can better be regarded as a tendential development – between Industrial and Information Warfare.

INDUSTRIAL WARFARE

Industrial Warfare, which may be said to have characterized the period from around 1914[7] through the 1960s and into the 1970s, has the following attributes:

- War was conducted, for the most part, between nation states and chiefly concerned disputes over territory.
- Mobilization of large elements of, and indeed entire, populations was undertaken to support the war effort. This involved major changes in the labour force (most obviously women taking over occupations to release men of fighting age), and, of course, a related perception of civilian populations as targets by combatants (something that explains the enormous growth in civilian casualties of war in the twentieth century, dramatically illustrated in the 50 million deaths during the Second World War, most of them civilians (Gilbert, 1989, pp. 745–7)).
- Sustained efforts to dovetail industrial production and the military struggle, often involving quasi-nationalization, in a strategy of 'total war'.
- Participation, by historical standards, of huge numbers of combatants, something generally involving the conscription of a majority of males between the ages of 18 and about 34. Concomitantly, when these massed forces were put into action, mass casualties were sustained.
- Strenuous efforts to plan the war effort as a whole, something that extended from government takeover of industries, such as transport and energy, that were deemed essential to the war effort, through to elaborate and detailed strategies drawn up by high-ranking military commanders who would decide centrally how best to deploy their forces and then direct subordinates to implement that plan.
- Harnessing media to assist the war effort by laying emphasis on the national interest in moral and material terms, hence nurturing strong media commitment in support of the fighting forces and using, where necessary, national powers to censor and direct information.

INFORMATION WARFARE

Over the past generation or so we have seen the unravelling of Industrial Warfare, to be replaced, in an incremental but accelerating manner, by what one might term Information Warfare. There is a tendency to conceive this in somewhat narrow technological terms, hence the much discussed (Cohen, 1996) Revolution in Military Affairs (RMA). This evokes radical changes in military technologies, from the 'digital soldier' to the latest technologies involving drones, satellites and computer-drenched weapons of bewildering complexity. Enormous advances in technologies have been made, notably in aeronautics and electronics-rich weaponry, though applications from computer communications have come at an unprecedented rate since the late 1980s. Central to the RMA are developments in command, control, communications and intelligence (C3I) technologies, the pursuit of a first-rate system of one's own and identification of vulnerable points in the enemies' (Berkowitz, 2003). Ultra-sophisticated C3I networks can provide an enormous 'information advantage' in warfare, something that was highlighted in the *Economist*'s post-mortem of the 1991 Gulf War. Its correspondent concluded that:

> the key was the information advantage provided by a communications network that linked satellites, observation aircraft, planners, commanders, tanks, bombers, ships and much more. It enabled the allies to get around ... OODA (observation, orientation, decision and action) loops at breath-taking speed in a sort of continuous temporal outflanking. A completely new air-tasking order – a list of hundreds of targets for thousands of sorties – was produced every 72 hours, and would be updated even while the aircraft were airborne. Iraq's radar eyes were poked out, its wireless nerves severed. (Morton, 1995)

An integral constituent of C3I is, of course, surveillance systems, institutionalized in the US's National Security Agency (NSA) and the UK's Government Communications Headquarters (GCHQ) (Bamford, 2001). The reality and significance of RMA is unarguable, but I would wish to conceive Information Warfare in broader terms than the technological (Webster, 2001). Amongst its other distinguishing features are the following.

- Information Warfare no longer requires the mass mobilization of the population (at least not inside the major powers, where an important aim is to wage 'clean war' in which their own civilian population will be unscathed). Conduct of war will rely on relatively small numbers of professional soldiers, pilots and support teams. This represents a shift in the military towards what have been called 'knowledge warriors',[8] a term that underscores the centrality of personnel adept, not in close combat or even in riflemanship, but in handling complex and highly computerized tools such as advanced fighter aircraft, surveillance systems, and guidance technologies. This changing character of the military machine is consonant with what have been described as 'post-military societies' (Shaw, 1991) where war-fighting institutions have moved to the margins of society and have taken on more specialized and technically demanding roles, as well as with what Edward Luttwak has called a 'post-heroic' military policy where one's own side brings to bear overwhelming force on an enemy chiefly through bombing while few, if any, casualties are risked from one's own side (Luttwak, 1996).

- Following the collapse of the Soviet Union and the reduction of the attendant threat of a collision of superpowers, the expectation is that future conflicts will be what Manuel Castells terms 'instant wars' (Castells, 1996, pp. 454–61) by which is meant relatively brief encounters, with active operations lasting only for days or a few weeks, in which the United States (or NATO and/or UN approved forces) is victorious by virtue of overwhelming superiority of its military resources.

The Gulf Wars of 1991 and 2003, the Balkans War of 1999, and the Afghanistan battles of 2001, each of which lasted between just three and eleven weeks, exemplify this feature. In the Gulf Wars the allied forces were insuperably better equipped and prepared than were the Iraqis,[9] and the consequences were evident in the brevity of the campaign and in the respective losses. In 1991 the American and British side lost a few hundred, while between 30,000 and 60,000 Iraqi troops perished, many of these on the 'Turkey Shoot' as they fled, under fire, back to Iraq on the Basra road, their country having endured 42 days of war in which, it has been estimated, more explosive power was delivered than during the whole of the Second World War (Mandeles, Hone & Terry, 1996, p. 24). The 'Shock and Awe' campaign of 2003 was devastatingly effective, leading to capitulation of the Iraqi forces after just weeks of massive and sustained bombing by 'smart' weapons, without a handful of British and American losses. The situation in Serbia during 1999 was broadly comparable. There was extreme reluctance to commit ground troops from the NATO alliance (and especially from the Americans themselves) for fear of taking casualties against which domestic opinion might rebel. Accordingly, the war was fought by NATO entirely from the air and, though a couple of aircraft were lost, there were no fatalities inflicted on the allies by the Serbian forces.[10] It appears that sustained air attack was sufficient for NATO to prevail (though knowledge of preparations for a ground invasion in early July 1999 may well have hastened Serbia's capitulation). In marked contrast to NATO emerging unscathed, intensive bombing of Serbia left between 5000 and 7000 dead. Of course, much the greatest number of fatalities was inflicted by the Serbian military and paramilitary forces who occupied Kosovo, creating some 800,000 ethnic Albanian refugees and an estimated 10,000 Kosovan deaths in 'Operation Horseshoe'. And in the war against the Taliban in Afghanistan over late 2001, despite the anxieties expressed beforehand (about hardened and fanatical warriors, in treacherous terrain and with heavy armaments), the war was rapidly brought to an end with minimal US loss and little soldier-to-soldier combat[11] (air attack dominated and the US enjoyed absolute supremacy).

• Information Warfare does not require either the mobilization of the citizenry or of industry for the war effort. It relies instead on capturing only leading edges of industrial innovation for military purposes – for instance, electronic engineering, computing, telecommunications and aerospace. To this extent Information Warfare represents a reduction in the militarization of society, though it necessarily has an important presence in cutting-edge innovations.

• Information Warfare requires meticulous planning, but this is planning for flexibility of response, in contrast to the much more elaborate and cumbersome plans of the Industrial Warfare period. Today enormous volumes of information flows, along with the incorporation of software into weapons themselves, feed into complex planning for war, which prioritizes 'mobility, flexibility, and rapid reaction' (Secretary of State for Defence, 1996, para. 171). A recurrent theme now is that the military should have flexibility to 'swarm' into troubled regions, to converge at speed from various points to attack enemies that are also likely to be dispersed. Game theory, simulations (frequently using sophisticated video facilities), and the production of systems are integral elements of Information Warfare, as is the necessity to plan on the basis of the 'certainty of uncertainty' (Oettinger, 1990). There are many examples of this capability, from the presence of AWACS (Airborne Warning and Control Systems) planes, continuously off the ground, which monitor huge areas in detail, then pinpoint targets for precision attacks from back-up forces, to the capacity, during the Afghanistan battles, for air command in Saudi Arabia to deliver B52 strikes within 19 minutes to Afghanistan after receiving coordinates from special forces on the ground (Ignatieff, 2002).

• The removal of the civilian population to the margins of the day-to-day conduct of Information Warfare, and the reliance on expert 'knowledge warriors', has profound implications for the experiences of war. On the one hand, without mass mobilization, the general population has little direct involvement with information war, even when this is undertaken in its name. On the other hand, the general population has a very much expanded second-hand experience of warfare, in the particular sense of massively increased media coverage of conflicts (of which more below). That is, while in Information Warfare the fighting units are at the margins of society, media coverage is massive and a most important and intrusive dimension of the wider public's experiences of war.

- It follows that Information Warfare must devote great attention to 'perception management' of the population at home and, indeed, round the world. This is especially pressing in democratic nations where public opinion is an important factor in the war effort and where a genuine fear for military leaders is a concerted domestic reaction against the war, since this may seriously impinge on the fighting capability of their forces. Further, there is widespread apprehension that the public will react to vivid pictures of the wrong sort (say bloodied bodies of innocent civilians rather than 'precision strikes on legitimate targets'). Inevitably, this impels military leaders into careful rehearsals and management of information from and about the war, though at the same time assiduous efforts must be made to avoid the charge of censorship, since this flies in the face of democratic states having a 'free media' and undermines the persuasiveness of what does get reported. Perception management must therefore attempt to combine ways of ensuring a continuous stream of media coverage that is positive and yet ostensibly freely gathered by independent news agencies.[12] Some have suggested that coverage of the Gulf War in 1991 evidenced especially effective 'perception management', since it achieved massive media attention yet was antiseptic in substance (Smith, 1992; Mowlana, Gerbner & Schiller, 1992; Taylor, 1992; Bennett & Paletz, 1994). To this degree Jean Baudrillard's (1991) proclamation that the 'Gulf War never happened' is correct, in so far as the television and media coverage was managed most adroitly by the military allies. Later engagements in Kosovo and Afghanistan, and again in Iraq were more problematical.

INFORMATION WARFARE, HUMAN RIGHTS AND MEDIA

Here I want to focus attention on the media dimensions of present-day Information Warfare. It is obvious that combatants desire to have media on board, so that what happens in war is presented in ways that are acceptable to the wider public. However, for reasons I have already discussed, 'perception management' is difficult to achieve, chiefly because strict control

of the media in an era of globalization is, to say the least, problematic when there are thousands of journalists present, when
they define their role as primarily an investigative activity, when
domestic dissent is sure to get some coverage in democratic
regimes, and where technologies, from video cameras to the
Internet, mean that images, reports and opinions are relatively
easily gathered and communicated.

But the media are needed for more than reporting acceptable
news from the battlefield. They are also central players in
justifying war itself, again this is especially so in democracies.
The public may only be spectators in Information Warfare, but
interventions need to be legitimated and, in today's world, this
is considerably more difficult than in the period of Industrial
Warfare, when the nation at war, for national interests, could
harness national media to its war ends. On the one hand, this
legitimation is essential because withdrawal of public support
means that the fighting forces are weakened in their efforts. On
the other hand, this need to gain public support in democratic
societies is a key point of entry for consideration of 'human
rights regimes', for the spread of what has been called 'cosmopolitan democracy'. And this is, necessarily, something in
which media are involved, not merely as conduits for opinions
of military or government leaders (though doubtless this is
present), but as surveillance agencies that examine and explore
the democratic bases for interventions from outside. It appears to
me that this was a distinguishing feature of the media's part in
both wars with Iraq, the Kosovan War of 1999, and the
Afghanistan intervention of 2001.

Furthermore, the foregoing suggests that media come to play
a role in Information Warfare only after conflict has commenced.
But media are present before this stage and can play a key role in
'shaming' regimes by exposing poor human rights records and
in instigating intervention in certain areas. I do not wish to oversimplify the situation, but it seems to me that, in an appreciable
if hard to measure manner, there has developed an increased sen-
sitivity towards, and awareness of, 'human rights' and their
abuses around the world (Robertson, 1999; Held, 1995). This is
connected to a range of factors, not the least of which is the
steady deepening of democracy around the world (Human Development Report, 2002), though always media are intimately

involved. The spread of news reportage and television docu-
mentaries is crucial, but so too is the massive extension of foreign
travel, as well as organizations such as Amnesty International,
UNICEF, Human Rights Watch, the Red Cross and Médecins Sans
Frontières (cf. Urry, 1999).

Of course these do not act with a
single purpose, and neither do they transmit messages of a
uniform kind, but I think, nevertheless, that they do engender a
sentiment that human beings have universal rights – of freedom
from persecution and torture, of religious toleration, of self-deter-
mination, of access to resources such as food and water, and so
on (Ghandhi, 2002; Brownlie & Goodwin-Gill, 2002). Doubtless
it will be objected that this commitment to 'human rights' is
vague, inconsistent and inchoate. Even were this so, it does not
weaken the commitment, which can, in appropriate circumstances, lead to calls that 'something should be done' – whether
about starving children, victims of disasters, or even about those
oppressed by military aggressors.

In addition, the connected processes of accelerated globalization (which itself plays a key role in heightening awareness of
'human rights') and the collapse of communism have weakened
nation states and encouraged a more global orientation in which
universal rights are more important than hitherto. This
represents a significant break with established practices where
emphasis has been placed on the territorial integrity of nations.
Appalling things might be happening to citizens inside a nation,
but to date it has been exceedingly difficult to envisage other
governments, so long as their own borders and/or interests were
not threatened, intervening out of concern for victims within
another's sovereign territory. Even today it is not easy to get
international forces to invade others' national frontiers. There
was a period in the United States, after losing 18 military
personnel in Somalia late in 1993, when President Clinton
withdrew his forces and vowed not to put them at risk again
(Power, 2002). It is possible, for instance, that NATO's involvement in Kosovo would not have happened but for the horrific
recent history of Bosnia, itself given saturation media coverage,
and perhaps most notably the slaughter by the Serbian militia of
up to 7000 Muslim men and adolescent boys who surrendered
at Srebrenica in July 1995.[13] At the same time, neither the NATO
involvement in Kosovo during the spring and early summer of

1999, nor the British entry into Sierra Leone in 2000, can be explained satisfactorily in terms of the strategic, still less territorial, interests that dominated military decision-making in the days of the supreme nation state. These latter have of course by no means disappeared, as the 'realist' advice at the time – to stay out of areas where ancient ethnic hatreds prevailed and where no self-interest was evident – testifies.[14]

Václav Havel (1999) articulated the changed situation when he voiced support for the NATO engagement in Kosovo on the grounds that 'the notion that it is none of our business what happens in another country and whether human rights are violated in that country ... should ... vanish down the trapdoor of history'. Tony Blair (2001), much more directly involved, made the same case for intervention to bring down the Taliban regime in Afghanistan. Evoking the 'interdependence (which) defines the new world we live in', Blair defended intervention on grounds of democracy and human rights:

> When Milosevic embarked on the ethnic cleansing of Muslims in Kosovo, we acted. The sceptics said it was pointless, we'd make matters worse, and we'd make Milosevic stronger. And look what happened: we won, the refugees went home, the policies of ethnic cleansing were reversed and one of the great dictators of the last century will see justice in this century. And I tell you if Rwanda happened again today as it did in 1993, when a million people were slaughtered in cold blood, we would have a moral duty to act there also. We were there in Sierra Leone when a murderous group of gangsters threatened its democratically elected government and people.

Of course, one cannot be blind to the fact that nation states remain important and that realpolitik concerns will continue to tell when it comes to questions of intervention of forces from outside (see Hirst, 2001). One may think, in this light, of how hard it is to imagine outside intervention in China in support of democratizing forces: though that nation is a police state, it is also in possession of nuclear weapons and mighty military resources. Nonetheless, it still seems to be the case that Information Warfare must unavoidably be concerned with much more than strategic or territorial interests, precisely because the informational elements of organized violence are nowadays critical and hard to contain. And a key feature of these elements is the spread of a universalism that denies the right of nations to do as they will inside their own borders and media (as well as other agencies and actors) surveillance of events which ensure that nations cannot easily hide from outside scrutiny. Again to quote Havel (1999), it would 'seem that the ... efforts of generations of democrats ... [a]nd the evolution of civilization have finally brought humanity to the recognition that human beings are more important than the state'. To be sure, it is likely that mendacious nations will continue to disguise territorial interests by adopting the language of 'human rights', but that such countries feel this is a useful legitimating strategy is itself testament to the spread of the human rights discourse, which, while national borders are of decreasing importance, may lead to interventions by transnational communities. It is the same drive that led to the holding of General Pinochet in Britain between 1998 and 2000 and his subsequent prosecution in Chile (he was released in 2001 on grounds of health), and the working of the United Nations War Crimes Tribunal in The Hague that has led to the conviction of numerous Serbian and other war criminals, up to and including Slobodan Milosevic and former Bosnian Serb president, Biljana Plavsic. In July 2002 an International Criminal Court, able to prosecute human rights abusers anywhere in the world, was opened by the United Nations in The Hague. Political leaders, army officers and any others suspected of crimes against humanity will be liable to be called to account.

CONCLUSION

What I have urged in this chapter is hesitancy in tracing a straightforward connection between surveillance, the nation state, war and a need to monitor enemies within and without the country. There is a lineage here, one that ought not to be ignored, but in my view it too readily pushes the subject of surveillance to the margins of social life. I have argued that the changed circumstances that surround the pursuit of Information Warfare, most notably globalization and a heightened role for media, mean that we need to see surveillance from a broader, as well as more differentiated, point of view. If we do this we can appreciate that, while media penetrate deep into everyday life and thereby inescapably impinge on our consciousnesses, they ought not to be seen simply as conduits of the military machine in times of war. On the contrary, whatever the efforts that are made to ensure effective 'perception management', the media are a good deal more complicated and play a more ambiguous part, when it comes to not just the conduct, but perhaps even the initiation of Information War.

NOTES

1. There is a remarkable instance of this described by David Halberstam, in which then President Lyndon Johnson woke CBS president Frank Stanton from his bed early one morning in 1965 with the question 'are you trying to fuck me?', whence he continued to tell Stanton that his 'boys' had 'just shat on the American flag' because they had screened a report from Vietnam that had filmed US marines burning a village (Halberstam, 1979, p. 490).
2. Howard Tumber (2002) prefers the term 'trench coat culture', suggesting machismo rather than heroism.
3. For instance, in the Afghanistan battles late in 2001, eight journalists were killed compared with seven United States soldiers. And in the spring of 2002 news came from Israel of the killing by Israeli soldiers of Italian photojournalist Raffaele Ciriello in Ramallah. At the same time journalists from France and Egypt were injured by shooting and shrapnel, and the *Guardian* (March 14, 2002) reported that at least 40 foreign journalists have been shot by Israeli live and rubber bullets during the intifada that began in autumn 2000. Similarly the *New York Times* (March 27, 2002) reported 37 journalists killed during 2001 as a direct result of their work. Numerous journalists lost their lives in the 2003 Iraq War, and the Israeli/Palestinian conflict continues to produce casualties amongst correspondents – in May 2003 (time of writing) film maker James Miller was shot dead by Israeli troops.
4. Cees Hamelink draws on United Nations research to note that 25 per cent of the world's poor does not benefit from economic growth, that the poorest 25 per cent share only 1.4 per cent of world income, and that over 1 billion people live on less than 1 dollar per day (Hamelink, 2000).
5. And not all undesirable. See, for example, Benjamin Barber (1995) and Christopher Lasch (1995).
6. Elsewhere we find instances of fundamentalist creeds that urge 'ethnic cleansing' of 'aliens' in the name of a mythic nation – on the way fighting what have been called 'degenerate wars' in regions that have been hard hit by instabilities exacerbated by recent trends (Kaldor, 1999)
7. Of course the date 1914 is imprecise and Industrial Warfare has origins further back in time. Nef (1950), for instance, traces the commencement of mass armies using industrially produced weapons to the Napoleonic era.

8. Military thinking is much influenced by the thinking of Alvin and Heidi Toffler, who coined the term 'knowledge warriors' (Toffler & Toffler, 1993). The Tofflers have also written a foreword to a recent influential book on information war (Arquilla & Ronfeldt, 1997).

9. Several commentators have wondered whether the 1991 victory would have been quite so easy against a more robust enemy than Iraq. See, for example, Mandeles, Hone & Terry (1996). Expectations that in 2003 circumstances would be much more difficult for the US/British forces were confounded. It appears that their overwhelmingly superior weaponry devastated even the experienced and elite Iraqi Republican Guard.

10. There were two American pilots killed when an Apache helicopter crashed during a training exercise. *Guardian*, June 11, 1999.

11. As of March 9, 2002 there were 14 US servicemen's deaths.

12. The refusal of Israel to allow journalists into the occupied territories while its forces engaged with Palestinians, notably in Jenin, early in 2002 was a tactic that – while it removed reporters who might have uncovered issues and events embarrassing to the Israeli Defence Force – inevitably raises questions about Israel's capacity to win the 'information war' in the Middle East, though that country is overwhelmingly superior in terms of weaponry to any potential enemies. An outcome has been the airing of the strongest criticism of the Jewish state in British media in 50 years.

13. It is also remarkable to note that, when the Netherlands Institute for War Documentation reported, in April 2002, on the ineptitude of the Dutch troops' peacekeeping role at Srebrenica, the entire government felt compelled to resign.

14. I concede that the response in 1991 to the Iraqi invasion of Kuwait was at least in part motivated by a US interest in securing its oil supplies. It has also been agreed that the security of oil reserves played a major part in instigating the 2003 invasion of Iraq, and that to this degree it was a typically colonial affair. I find this unpersuasive, not least because of the current surplus of energy that is available. However, the primary rationale offered for the war – to locate and disable weapons of mass destruction – looks flimsy in view of the difficulties experienced in locating them and in evidence that the Iraqi regime was being successfully contained prior to the invasion. It is unclear precisely what led to the 2003 war. Doubtless the destruction of the Twin Towers on September 11, 2001 played a part, as did the aggressively right-wing politics of George Bush's government (though the war is likely to have achieved little in the 'battle against terrorism'). Prime Minister Blair, in response to the largest-ever anti-war protest in Britain in February 2003, did articulate the human rights case for intervention, and the nastiness of Saddam Hussein's rule is beyond dispute, though such reasoning was subordinated during the crisis.

7
Mapping out Cybercrimes in a Cyberspatial Surveillant Assemblage

David S. Wall

Perhaps the most transformative aspect of the Internet is its capability to foster networks of interaction that are distributed across almost infinite spans of space, whilst also converging a range of different information technologies. Significant here is the fact that the networks generate multiple information flows that are also multi-directional, thus providing levels and types of connectivity not previously experienced by communications technologies. The Internet is not simply a 'super' (Poster, 1995), 'virtual' (Engberg, 1996) or 'electronic' (Lyon, 1994, ch. 4) Panopticon: an extension of Foucault's conceptualization of Bentham's prison design – 'seeing without being seen' (Foucault, 1983, p. 223), as has become the conventional wisdom. It is important to emphasize that Internet information flows are simultaneously *panoptic* and *synoptic* – not only can the few watch the many, but the many can watch the few (Mathieson, 1997, p. 215). The multi-directional informational flow helps to make the Internet a distinctive 'surveillant assemblage' (Haggerty & Ericson, 2000, p. 605) with an 'idolatrous dream of omniperception' and a 'minacious twinkle in the electronic eye' (Lyon, 2001a, p. 147). These processes can create enormous benefits for society, but the same processes also create opportunities for new and distinctive forms of criminal and harmful behaviours. Mapping out these behaviours to provide further understanding of cybercrimes will be the focus of this chapter.

It will be argued here that, for a number of rational reasons, popular understandings of cybercrimes tend to fixate upon harmful behaviours that have common points of reference in existing statutes and crime agendas. The 'true' cybercrimes are quite distinct from traditional criminal activities carried out on the Internet in that they are characterized by its distributed and multi-directional surveillant qualities that are made possible by the convergence of information technologies. The subsequent analysis and discussion will contribute to the 'new politics of surveillance' that has emerged during the past decade and which was further shaped by the political aftermath of September 11 2001 (see Lyon, 2001b).

The first part of this chapter will explore briefly the existing problems of understanding cybercrimes before mapping out the cybercrime terrain. The second part will consider in some detail the transformative aspects of the Internet upon criminal behaviours. The third part, before concluding, briefly outlines the role of the production of criminological knowledge in the 'cybercrime' agenda, which has shaped debates over cybercrimes.

UNDERSTANDING AND MAPPING OUT CYBERCRIMES

A major impediment to the development of current understandings of cybercrime is the popular rubric that tends to confuse both traditional and non-traditional criminal activities, thereby hindering the production of empirical knowledge about it. Furthermore, without systematic clarification of the nature of cybercrimes, dystopian, and often inept concerns about them can result in misplaced or exaggerated public demands for policy responses from criminal justice agencies.

'Cybercrime' is a term that now symbolizes insecurity in cyberspace. Yet, in itself, the term is fairly meaningless, other than signifying the occurrence of a harmful behaviour that is computer mediated or enabled. More importantly, it is largely an invention of the media and has no specific reference point in law; in fact, many of the so-called cybercrimes are not necessarily crimes in law, they are harms. Brenner actually questions whether or not 'there are indeed such things as cybercrimes' (2001, p. 11). However, although the term 'cyberspace crime' would probably be a more precise and accurate descriptor, 'cybercrime' has acquired considerable linguistic agency. Furthermore, in recent years cybercrimes have become embedded into the public crime agenda as 'something that must be policed'.

While there is common agreement that cybercrimes exist, there appears to be little common understanding as to what they are (Wall, 2001, p. 168). Many attempts have been made to define cybercrimes, for example, 'computer mediated activities which are either illegal or considered illicit by certain parties, and which can be conducted through global economic networks' (Thomas & Loader, 2000, p. 3) or the occurrence of a harmful behaviour that is related to a networked computer (see NCIS, 1999a). These definitions indicate the networked and global nature of the cybercrime problem and, importantly, they also indicate that both offender and victims must be online. But these definitions do not tell us much about the transformative aspects of the Internet upon criminal and harmful behaviours.

Mapping out the cybercrime terrain

An analysis of the behaviours referred to as cybercrimes by the news media, academics and others illustrates a matrix of cybercrime in which levels of impact upon opportunities for offending are mapped against types of offending behaviour (see further Wall, 2002a, p. 192). The matrix begins to demonstrate the complexities of cybercrime and enables criminological debates to start to focus upon the implications for policing, crime prevention and crime control. Perhaps more importantly, the matrix also provides a useful tool for exploring the ways that the Internet has shaped criminal behaviours (see Table 7.1).

The Internet has both increased the efficiency of the administration and organization of some types of crime and their perpetration and created entirely new opportunities for old and new criminal behaviours. These impacts manifest themselves in three key ways, which are outlined below.

First, the Internet has made more efficient the perpetration of 'traditional' criminal activities that are currently the subject of existing criminal or civil law. The new forms of communications that the Internet creates and the relative anonymity that it permits have, for example, enabled drug dealers to conclude their deals by e-mail. The same communications networks can also assist in the planning and maintenance of organized criminal operations. However, it is important to stress that were networked communication technologies suddenly not to exist,

Table 7.1: The Matrix of Cybercrimes – level of impact by type of crime with selected examples

Crime type Impact level	Trespass/Access/Harm	Acquisition (Theft/Deception)	Obscenity/ Pornography	Violence/Hate
Facilitating traditional crime	Phreaking/Cracking/ Hacking	Frauds/Pyramid schemes	Trading sexual materials	Stalking
New opportunities for engaging in traditional crime	Issue based hactivism/ protest/ Cyber-vandalism	Multiple frauds/Trade secret thefts	Online sex trade/ Child pornography	Hate speech campaigns/ Organized paedophile rings
New opportunities for new types of criminal behaviour	Information warfare/Cyber-terrorism	Intellectual property piracy/Gambling/ Information theft/ Identity theft	Cyber-sex/ Cyber-pimping	Organized weapons talk/Drug talk

Source: Wall, 2002a, p. 192 – subsequently amended

115

these same types of criminal activity would probably still occur through the use of other means of communication.

Second, the Internet has provided offenders with a range of new opportunities for committing 'traditional' criminal activities on a global scale. Examples of these 'hybrid' criminal activities might include the global trade in sexually explicit materials; the proliferation of multiple frauds and other economic crimes (see Grabosky & Smith, 2001, p. 30; Levi, 2001, p. 44); online protest against the www sites of online organizations, such as hate speech campaigns, issue-based hactivism; and globally organized paedophile abuse rings. In short, without the Internet these criminal activities would exist but not on such a global scale. They are also characterized by a symmetry in the relationship between the offender and the victim; and by a degree of consensus about the nature of the offence.

Third, the Internet has created some entirely new criminal opportunities which have generated novel forms of behaviour – the 'true' cybercrimes – on a global scale. Like the hybrid cybercrimes, these activities simply would not exist without Internet technologies. But unlike the hybrid cybercrimes, these activities are the specific product of the Internet. Typically characterized by a lack of symmetry and clarity in the relationship between the offender and the victim, they also lack the consensual under-standing of the nature of the offence that is found with traditional crimes. Examples would include the unauthorized acquisition of intellectual property; the piracy of software tools, music and film products (see further Wall, 2001, p. 3); informa-tion warfare and cyber-terrorism (Walker, 2002, ch. 1); but most importantly the various deceptive and harmful payloads distrib-uted by unsolicited bulk e-mails (UBEs) (Wall, 2002b).

In practice, cybercrimes will often display aspects of each of the above, and the latterly mentioned unsolicited bulk e-mails (UBEs) (or spamming) provide a good example. Not only are UBEs super-efficient methods for offenders to ensnare victims, they can also constitute crimes in themselves, as can the unpleasant payloads they deliver. Furthermore, they can simul-taneously convey information about the victim to the offender and about the offender to the victim. Spamming is discussed later in greater detail.

Types of cybercrime

The very qualities of the Internet that have popularized it have also engendered new criminal opportunities. So, not only has the Internet had different levels of impact upon criminal behaviour, it has also fostered specific groups of offending behaviour, which are currently raising public concern (discussed more fully in Wall, 1999; 2001, p. 3). Each of these 'cybercrime' groups suggests a range of behaviours rather than specific offences, although they do reflect specific courses of public debate and respective areas of law. They are trespass; acquisition (theft and deception); obscenity (pornography); and violence/hate.

Trespass or hacking/cracking, is the unauthorized access of computer systems where rights of ownership or title have already been established. A distinction is increasingly being made in the literature between the principled trespasser – the hacker – and the unprincipled trespasser – the cracker (Taylor, 2001, p. 61). In its least harmful form, cyber-trespass is an intellectual challenge that results in a harmless trespass. In its most harmful manifestation, it is full-blown information warfare between social groups or even nation states. Somewhere between these positions falls the cyber-vandal, spy and terrorist (Wall, 1999).

Acquisition and deception. Often referred to as cyber-theft, this category describes the different types of acquisitive harm that can take place in cyberspace. At one level, there are the more traditional patterns of theft, such as the fraudulent use of credit cards and (cyber-) cash, and of particular public concern is the raiding of online bank accounts through deceptive behaviour. At another level, as values are increasingly attached to ideas rather than physical property (Barlow, 1994), new forms of electronic service theft are proliferating as offenders are drawn by the fact that customers are more willing than ever to pay for the consumption of online information services that include TV, music, film, legal information, news etc. Acts such as cyber-piracy (the appropriation of intellectual properties), identity theft and information theft (Wall, 1999) are causing us to reconsider our understanding of property and therefore the act of theft because there is no intention to permanently deprive.

Pornography/obscenity, is the trading of sexually expressive materials within cyberspace. The cyber-pornography/obscenity debate is very complex because the consumption or possession of pornography is not necessarily illegal. The test in the UK and other jurisdictions is whether or not the materials are obscene and deprave the viewer, but there are considerable legal and moral differences as to what the criteria are that enable law enforcers to establish obscenity and depravation (Chatterjee, 2001, p. 78). In Britain, for example, individuals might consume risqué images through the various facets of the mass media that might be considered obscene in some Middle Eastern countries, and yet are deemed perfectly acceptable in more permissive countries (Wall, 1999).

Violence/hate describes the violent impact of the cyber-activities of the perpetrator upon an individual, or a social or political grouping. Whilst such activities do not require a direct physical manifestation, the victim will nevertheless *feel* the violence of the act and may bear long-term psychological scars. The activities referred to here range from cyber-stalking by an individual, to hate speech where hate is circulated through news groups, to 'weapons-talk' where news groups discuss the technical aspects of weapons, their manufacture and procurement (Wall, 1999). Also included in the Violence/hate category is the child abuse that takes place as the result of the creation of child pornography.

TRANSFORMATIVE IMPACTS OF THE INTERNET ON CRIMINAL BEHAVIOURS

At this point it is useful to contrast traditional criminal activity with cyber-criminal activity, albeit drawing quite crude comparisons. Broadly speaking, traditional criminal activity displays some fairly characteristic and commonly understood features (Gottfredson & Hirschi, 1990; Braithwaite, 1992). First, it relates to the consensual or core values within a society as to what does or does not constitute a crime and these shared values are usually defined in criminal law. Second, criminal activities tend to take place in real time because their time frame is largely determined by the physical world, for example, having to take account of the speed of transport, the physical size of the haul, the needs of the offenders involved. Third, the majority of offending and victimization tends to take place within a distinct geographical boundary – especially in a sea-locked island like Great Britain.

Fourth, the criminology of traditional crime tends to be based on the offender, rather than the victim or the offence. Fifth, serious frauds notwithstanding, much of the debate over traditional crime has tended to focus upon working-class subcultures.

In contrast, cybercrimes exhibit almost the opposite characteristics. As indicated earlier, they are contentious in that there does not yet exist a core set of values about them. They are largely free of a physical time frame and therefore relatively, though not totally, instantaneous. Cybercrimes can also be transnational, trans-jurisdictional and global, and if there is a topography of the Internet, it is expressed more in terms of levels of access to the Internet and also language, rather than physical geography. The discussion of cybercrimes has tended to be offence-, rather than victim- or offender-based and, finally, cybercrimes tend to cover a broad range of legal issues, many of which are the subject of civil law in addition to, or instead of, the criminal law, demonstrating a resonance with the study of white-collar crime.

It is the traditional model of crime that tends to underpin the criminal justice paradigm and which informs understanding, and this highlights the need for a further examination of cybercrimes. As suggested above, two main, and potentially conflicting, types of information flow are discernible that are significant to the cybercrime debate. The first is the multi-directional (surveillant) flow of information that facilitates a wide range of new criminal opportunities on the Internet in terms of offender motivation and ability to reach possible victims across jurisdictions. The second type of information flow, a result of the distributed nature of the Internet, is that contained within individual networks; these multiple information flows obfuscate the production of criminological knowledge about cybercrimes, as will be shown in the next part of the chapter.

Multi-directional information flows

As stated earlier, the origins of true cybercrimes lie in the Internet's multi-directional information flows, which shape, or discipline, the behaviour of offenders, victims and those involved in policing the Internet who fall under its panoptic and synoptic gaze.

Multi-directional information flows encourage new forms of offender motivation. Further, the Internet's powerful information technologies have rationalized the criminal process to provide offenders with very efficient and powerful tools that enable them to operate globally. The little factual knowledge about offenders that does exist from reported cases, suggests that offenders are not the burly stereotypes of the streets, rather, they are more likely to share a broad range of social characteristics. The published examples of hacking cases and other Internet-related offences reported in the media draw a picture of hackers, crackers and fraudsters as young, fairly lonely and introverted, yet clever individuals, who are more likely of middle-class origin and often without prior criminal records. They possess expert knowledge and are motivated by a variety of financial and non-financial goals – though it is very likely, however, that offender profiles will vary according to the type of crime. Thus the far reach of Internet information flows enables offending at a distance with no direct engagement with victims, which is an attraction to the introverted who eschew face to face contact. The law enforcer's worst nightmare is the 'empowered small agent' (see Pease, 2001, p. 22) who can, from a distance, conduct information warfare, cyber-terrorism or acts with catastrophic implications.

An interesting augmentation of the hacker stereotype is provided by one of the most notorious hackers of the 1990s, Kevin Mitnick. Mitnick's profile, as outlined in his autobiography, indicates that the above description applied mainly during his formative years and his greatest 'hacking' accomplishments were actually achieved or greatly assisted by his mastery of *The Art of Deception* (the title of his 2002 book). He obtained technical information about security measures not through hacking skills but through what he calls 'social engineering', from key personnel working in the systems that he was targeting. Yet, it was still the multi-directional information flow capability that ultimately enabled Mitnick to practice his skills and crimes.

As the offender's reach is globalized then so the body of possible victims includes all of those who are online. There is frequent confusion over who the victims of cybercrime are, and the manner of their victimization, not only because victims can vary from individuals to social groups, but the harms done to them can range from the perceived to the actual. In cases such as cyber-stalking or the theft of cyber-cash, victimization is very much focused upon an individual, yet in other cases such as cyber-piracy or cyber-spying/terrorism, the impact of victimization is usually directed towards corporate or governmental bodies. Similarly, the focus of hate crimes tends to be upon minority groups. Moreover, as has been found with the reporting of white-collar crimes, it is likely that many victims of cybercrimes, be they primary or secondary victims, individuals or organizations, may be unwilling to acknowledge that they have been victimized, or, at least, it may take them some time before they realize it. At a personal level, this could arise because of embarrassment, ignorance of what to do or just simply 'putting it down to experience'. Alternatively, where victimization has been implied by a third party upon the basis of an ideological, political, moral or commercial assessment of risk, the victim or victim group may simply be unaware that they have been victimized or may even believe that they have not been victimized, as is the case in some of the debates over pornography on the Internet.

For corporate victims, fear of the negative commercial impact of adverse publicity greatly reduces their willingness to report their victimization to the police. Of importance here is the observation that the model of criminal justice that the police and other public law enforcement agencies offer to corporate victims is not generally conducive to their business interests (Goodman, 1997, p. 486). For these reasons, corporate victims tend to operate a 'private model' of justice that furthers the corporate, rather than the public, interest. Put simply, corporate victims prefer to sort out their own problems by using their own resources in ways that are more likely to meet their own particular ends. Even where prosecutions are forthcoming, corporate bodies tend to favour civil recoveries rather than criminal prosecutions because of the lesser burden of proof and because they feel that they can maintain a greater control over the justice process. Alternatively, they might find it easier to claim for losses through insurance, or simply to pass on the costs of victimization directly to their customers.

It is typical of the Internet's universality that the very same multi-directional quality that extends the offender's reach to victims on a global scale can also, in principle, allow those same victims to surveille offenders, and so too can those who police the Internet. To assist with this function there exists a range of tools and facilities that enable individuals to gain information about the identities of those who are sending them messages. Furthermore, records exist of all traffic that takes place over the Internet and, in many jurisdictions, Internet service providers are required by law to retain their traffic data for specified periods of time, thus making the Internet an extremely efficient surveillant tool. The same qualities contribute to what Haggerty and Ericson have referred to in their broader discussion of the surveillant assemblage as 'the disappearance of disappearance', (2000, p. 619).

However, the use of Internet collection of Internet traffic data relies upon the integrity and accuracy of input data and its maintenance. Information is not always kept by Internet service providers and where the information exists there may not be the resources to pay for data mining. Online identities and identifiers can still easily be masked, which further frustrates policing and requires the expenditure of additional resources. Furthermore, while there now exists a range of privacy laws in Europe and the US, the majority of the online community appear willing to give up their privacy as long as they receive something in return (see Poster, 1995; Haggerty & Ericson, 2000).

Other practical policing problems include trans-jurisdictionality, which creates three specific problems for policing. The first problem is that of resource management, because policing strategies are often reduced to decisions that are made at a very local level over the most efficient expenditure of finite resources (Goodman, 1997, p. 486). Such decisions become complicated where different jurisdictions cover the location of the offence committed, the offender, victim and impact of the offence. The second problem is the effective investigation of crimes. Most policing tends to be based upon local and 'routinized' practices that define occupational cultures and working patterns. Thus, investigative difficulties tend to arise when non-routine events occur such as cross-border investigations, or types of behaviour that are not normally regarded as criminal by police officers (Reiner, 2000; Wall, 1997, p. 223). The third problem is located where the harms fall under civil laws in one jurisdiction and criminal law in another. One example is the theft of trade secrets, which is a criminal offence in the US, but not in the UK. In the

UK, only the manner by which the theft takes place can be criminal (see Law Commission, 1997).

The impact of multi-directional information flows – the example of spamming

In the absence of systematic knowledge about cybercrimes, the public have come to rely upon news media coverage and the opinions of professional security 'experts'. As a consequence, public understanding is easily shaped by the media focus upon sensational 'what if' scenarios, based as it is upon responses to media reporting of a few, usually dramatic cases. Therefore perceptions of cybercrime tend to be shaped by, on the one hand, fear of assault upon the fabric of society through cyber-terrorism, information warfare and paedophilia and, on the other hand, personal vulnerability, the fear of unwittingly become victim to identity theft, frauds, stalking etc. All of these threats are quite real and cases exist, so it would be wrong to say that they did not exist. However, what we do not yet know with much accuracy is the probability of the threats. Therefore, the example of spamming, or the distribution of unsolicited bulk e-mail (UBEs), will be explored here as a cybercrime (drawn from Wall, 2002c). This choice is driven by the fact that spamming affects just about everyone online, yet it is rarely discussed as anything other than a hindrance when in fact its impacts are felt quite broadly and in some cases very deeply.

Spamming is so called because UBEs are 'something that keeps repeating ... to great annoyance', as in Monty Python's 'Spam Song' wherein the term 'spam' was sung repeatedly by a group of Vikings in a restaurant (*Compuserve*, 1997; Edwards, 2000, p. 309; Khong, 2001). UBEs are e-mail advertisements that contain announcements about, and invitations to participate in, nefarious ways to earn money; obtain products and services free of charge; win prizes; ways to spy upon others; obtain improvements to health or well-being through revolutionary ways to lose weight, replace lost hair, increase one's sexual prowess or cure cancer.

There are some vague arguments in favour of UBEs, mostly upholding rights to free expression, but the demerits of UBEs override because of the overwhelming evidence that they generally degrade the quality of life of Internet users and invade the sanctity of individuals' privacy. UBEs rarely live up to their promises, often carrying unpleasant payloads in the form of either potent deceptions or viruses, worms or Trojans. UBEs not only choke up Internet bandwidth and slow down access rates, reducing efficiency, they also waste the time of Internet service providers and individual users through having to manage UBEs and deal with the computer viruses that they often carry. Rather worrying is the prediction, supported by empirical observations (Wall, 2002c) and other commentaries (Yaukey, 2001), that the problem of indiscriminate UBEs is likely to further increase during the coming years. UBEs should not simply be seen as a series of electronic mailshots, rather they are initiators of a potential two-way relationship, usually between offender and victim. At the heart of the UBE is a multi-directional information flow, without which any intended scams cannot be effected.

Spamming raises two important sets of concerns for the understanding of cybercrimes: the production of bulk e-mail lists and the impact of UBEs upon recipients. The first set of concerns relate to the spam industry, which is largely, though not exclusively, organized around the wholesale acquisition of online user's private information by surveilling Internet spiderbots. Individually, this private information, which typically comprises e-mail addresses, has no perceivable financial value, but it does when collated with 20 million or so other addresses. So, it is more than likely that the e-mail list, which provides the addresses to which the UBE is sent, was drawn from a CD-ROM of addresses sold to the spammer by a bulk e-mailer. The majority of e-mail addresses on the CD-ROMS are usually unconfirmed or unprofiled and therefore do not provide the spammer with the intended responses. Indeed, some of the main victims of spamming are the spammers themselves who have been duped into buying expensive CD-ROMS of unvalidated and useless e-mail addresses. Confirmed e-mail addresses have the higher value and are worth most when they are profiled by subject or owner characteristics because, like adverts, UBEs that contain information directly relevant to the recipient are the most likely to obtain a positive response and result in a transaction.

The purpose of many UBEs is therefore to elicit a response from the recipient from which the spammer can harvest valuable information. Typically, the e-mailshot may request an automatic response from the recipient's computer, or the subject matter may be either so offensive or ludicrous as to incite the recipient to 'flame' the sender. Another strategy is to invite the recipient in the content of the UBEs to 'deregister' from the e-mail list if they so wish. Some of these invitations themselves constitute 'remove.com' scams where the recipient innocently responds and subsequently becomes ensnared in a scam. In each case the spammer gains confirmation that the e-mail address is valid, and in the majority of cases also receives some important information about the recipient, which can include names, occupational information, business information, organization-specific domain names, signatures and so on.

The second set of concerns relates to the content and purpose of the UBE. The most pernicious threat from UBEs arises from the objectives of their content, which seeks either to engage victims in order to ensnare then entrap them in a fraudulent deception, or to persuade them to open an attachment that immediately loads spyware, or infects the recipient's computer with a virus, worm or Trojan. Before looking in more detail at the content of UBEs, it is important first to consider their impact upon recipients. Findings, drawn from the first two years of an ongoing longitudinal study of UBEs and their content, suggest that only a small proportion, possibly as low as 5–10 per cent of all UBEs, appeared to be legitimate attempts by vendors to inform the online public about their wares or to provide useful information. The remaining 90–95 per cent lacked reasonable commercial plausibility, thus supporting the finding that the majority of UBEs seek either to elicit a response or to deceive the recipient. Although this finding suggests a high level of risk to recipients, it says little about how they respond to the content of UBEs. An analysis of patterns of complaints about UBEs made by the online community to the network abuse department of a major telecommunications provider that hosts over 70 UK-based ISPs found that, although the receipt of (English language) UBEs is doubling annually, the percentage and overall number of complaints from online users about them is gradually falling over time (Wall, 2002b). This countervailing trend suggests that online communities are ceasing to regard UBEs as a threat and viewing them more as an incivility that can be coped with – usually by deleting. What is not certain, however, is how recipients respond to the increasingly sophisticated methods of seeking to attract their attention, for example by using plausible subject lines such as 'here is the information that you requested' or even including the first part of the recipient's e-mail address. Of even greater concern is the lack of knowledge about the ways that UBEs, their content and various payloads impact upon the more vulnerable groups within society. Major areas of concern are the retired, the poor, the redundant, single parents, those in remote locations, those with learning difficulties, the disadvantaged and others such as 'newbies' (newly online). The newly retired, for example, are particularly vulnerable to fraudsters because they seek ways to invest their retirement lump sums for their later years – the size of which they have never before previously possessed.

UBEs are now legally regulated in the EU, and therefore in the UK, under Article 13 (EU Directive, 2002). Article 13 of the Directive outlaws UBEs and prescribes that individuals have to 'opt in' to receive UBEs. Similarly, various US states have introduced a range of anti-spam laws. The problem is, however, that the spam industry exploits the trans-jurisdictionality of the Internet, which means that it continues to thrive. So, Article 13's effectiveness is likely to be limited, because although there has long been a need for anti-spam legislation in the UK and EU, most UBEs received in the UK originate in Korea and the West Coast of the US.

Table 7.2 illustrates the percentage breakdown of UBE contents and a more detailed typology of spam content follows. Though not an exact match, the categories and proportions equate roughly with Brightmail's 2002 survey entitled *Slamming Spam* (Brightmail, 2002).

Income-generating claims contain invitations to the recipient, supported by unsubstantiated claims, to take up or participate in lucrative business opportunities. Examples include the following sub-groups: a) investment reports and schemes; b) lucrative business opportunities such as pyramid selling schemes, ostrich farming schemes; c) earning money by working at home; d) Pump and Dump investment scams; e) Nigerian Advanced Fee scams; f) invitations to develop Internet sites and traffic for financial gains.

Table 7.2: UBE content received in one e-mail account 2000–01

	%
Income-generating claims	28
Pornography and materials with sexual content	16
Offers of free or discounted products, goods and services	15
Product adverts/information	11
Health cures/Snake oil remedies	11
Loans, credit options or repair credit ratings	9
Surveillance/Scares/Urban legends	5
Opportunities to win something, online gambling options	3
Other	2
Total	100

Source: Wall, 2002c

Pornography and materials with sexual content. Examples include the following sub-groups: a) straightforward invitations to gain access to an Internet site containing sexually explicit materials; b) invitations to join a group that is involved in sharing images and pictures about specific sexual activities; c) invitations to webmasters to increase traffic by including links to obtain access to sexually-oriented materials on their sites. Much of this is entrapment marketing, a theme common to many spams.

Offers of free or discounted products, goods and services (including free vacations). In order for recipients to be eligible for these offers they usually have to provide something in return, such as money, a pledge (via a credit card) or information about themselves, their family, their work or their lifestyle – often the hallmark of entrapment marketing. Examples include the following sub-groups: a) free products or services as long as the recipient signs up to the service, for example, for mobile phones, pagers, satellite TV. It is up to the recipient to withdraw from the service. The difference from normal 'free kit' marketing (Wall, 2000) is that the recipient is deceived into a binding agreement, or a non-existent or poorer quality service is provided, as has been the case with illegal telephone operations; b) spams that seek to exploit import tax or VAT differences between jurisdictions by selling items such as cheap cigarettes, alcohol, etc.; c) spams that sell goods from jurisdictions in which the goods are legal to those where the goods are either illicit or restricted, such as prescription medicines.

Advertisements/information about products and services. Some of these are genuine advertisements, others are blatantly deceptive. Examples include the following sub-groups: a) advertisements for office supplies, especially print cartridges; b) advertisements for greatly discounted computing and other equipment; c) advertisements selling medical supplies and equipment; d) advertisements for branded goods at greatly discounted prices; e) the sale of qualifications from unknown educational institutions; f) Internet auction scams whereby an advertisement containing information about the auction is spammed; g) the sale of bulk e-mail lists.

Health cures/Snake oil remedies. Spammers who send out UBEs advertising health cures or snake oil remedies seek to prey on vulnerable groups like the sick, elderly, poor and inadequate. Examples include the following sub-groups: a) miracle diets; b) anti-ageing lotions and potions; c) the illegal provision of prescription medicines; d) expensive non-prescription medicines at greatly discounted prices (such as Viagra); e) hair-loss remedies etc.; f) various body enhancement lotions, potions or operations, including breast, penis, muscle enlargement or fat reduction etc.; g) cures for cancer.

Offers and invitations to take up loans, credit options or repair credit ratings. Examples include the following sub-groups: a) offers of instant and unlimited loans or credit facilities, instant mortgages, often without the need for credit checks or security; b) the repair of bad credit ratings; c) offers of credit cards with zero or very low interest; d) offers that purport to target and engage with people whose financial life, for various reasons, exists outside the centrally run credit-rating-driven banking system.

Surveillance information, software and devices. This category is hard to disaggregate from the mischief section (the two are included together in Table 7.2) because it is hard to tell whether the information and products are genuine or not. Examples include: a) scare stories about the ability of others to surveil their Internet use in order to scare the recipient into buying materials (book, software etc.) that contain information about how to combat Internet surveillance and 'find out what other people know' about them; b) encouraging recipients to submit their online access details, purportedly in order to find out what people know about them; c) recommending an Internet-based service for testing recipient's own computer security; d) encouraging recipients to purchase spyware that purports to equip them to undertake Internet surveillance on others: 'Install Spector on your PC and it will record EVERYTHING your spouse, kids and employees do on the Internet' <www.spectorsoft.com>.

Hoaxes/Urban legends/Mischief collections. Examples include: a) UBEs that appear to be informative and tell stories that perpetuate various urban legends; b) hoax virus announcements or hoaxes such as the 'Gullibility virus', which seek to convince recipients into believing that they have accidentally received a virus then provides instructions on to how to remedy the problem, deceiving them in the process into removing a system file from their computer; c) messages which appear to be from friends, colleagues or other plausible sources that deceive the recipients into opening an attachment which contains a virus or a worm; d) chain letters, which sometimes suggest severe consequences to the recipient if they do not comply, or they may engage the recipient's sympathy with a particular minority group or cause, for example, single-parent women, or women in general (the Sisterhood Chain Letter scam); e) e-mail-based victim-donation scams that emerged on the Internet soon after the events of September 11, 2001; f) invitations to donate funds to obscure religious-based activities or organizations; g) links to hoax Internet sites, such as Convict.Net, which originally started as a spoof site, but was so heavily subscribed by former convicts that it eventually became reality.

Opportunities to win something, online gambling options. Examples include the following sub-groups: a) notification that the recipient has won a competition and must contact the sender so that the prize can be claimed – or they might provide some information before the prize can be received; b) offers to enter a competition if information or money is provided; c) free lines of credit in new trial gambling Internet sites. Mostly these are various forms of entrapment marketing (see earlier).

Unsolicited bulk e-mails are a very good example of true cybercrime in that they are a very efficient vehicle for enabling offenders to engage in a broad range of small-impact multiple victimizations, but on a global scale. They are the product of the surveillance of online populations and exploit the panoptic and synoptic capabilities of the Internet.

THE PRODUCTION OF CRIMINOLOGICAL KNOWLEDGE AND THE 'CYBERCRIME' AGENDA

This chapter has so far illustrated the extreme range of cyber-crimes, from the mundane, almost invisible, everyday annoyance of UBEs and their payloads, as illustrated above, to high-profile cases of child pornography, online paedophile rings, information warfare and cyber-terrorism. Yet, they all equally exploit global information networks by using the tools of surveillance inherent in the technology of the Internet. In doing so, they are as much dependent upon the actions of private and public sector organizations as they are upon the individual. The very same tools of surveillance inherent in the technology of the Internet, and exploited by cyber-criminals, can also be used to police and investigate cybercrimes. But a consequence of this quality is the creation of multiple and discrete information flows which, for the reasons outlined below, hinder the production of systematic and reliable knowledge about cybercrimes which can inform policy, counter the impacts of media sensitization that misshape public opinion while also levelling the playing field in the power play for control over cyberspace.

Multiple information flows

There are currently about five main strata at which policing governance, in the broader sense, is being achieved within cyberspace. These are the Internet users and user groups; Internet Service Providers (ISPs); corporate security departments/organizations; state-funded non-police organizations; and state-funded public police organizations. These 'policing' networks and their role in the governance of the Internet are discussed more fully elsewhere (see Wall 2001, pp. 171–7); however, their significance for this chapter is the fact that each generates information about cybercrimes that flows through each of the networks, but rarely across them.

A useful example of the lack of flow across strata can be observed when victim reports of security breaches are compared with prosecutions. A range of competently conducted surveys from both sides of the Atlantic indicate considerably high levels of security breaches. In England and Wales, these high levels of reported victimization suggest high levels of offences falling under the Computer Misuse Act 1990, which protects victims against unauthorized access to computer material (s.1); unauthorized access with intent to commit or facilitate commission of further offences (s.2); unauthorized modification of computer material (s.3).

The UK Department of Trade and Industry's (DTI) recent *Information Security Breaches Survey 2002* found that '44% of UK businesses have suffered at least one malicious security breach in the past year, nearly twice as many as in the 2000 survey' (DTI, 2002, p. 1). Such a high level of victimization also reflects the experience in the US. During 2002, the Computer Emergency Response Team (CERT) at Carnegie Mellon University recorded about 100,000 incidents of security breaches. Another US source, the FBI/Computer Security Institute found in its *2002 Computer Crime and Security Survey* that 'Ninety percent of respondents (primarily large corporations and government agencies) detected computer security breaches within the last twelve months' (FBI/CSI 2002, p. 4). But these high levels of victimization contrast dramatically against the actual prosecution figures. During the first decade following its introduction (1991–2000) a total of 53 offenders had been cautioned under the Computer Misuse Act and a further 88 prosecuted. Of the prosecuted, 68 (77 per cent) were convicted; 15 under s.1, 11 under s.2 and 42 under s.3 (Source: Home Office Research Development and Statistics, Crime and Criminal Justice Unit – also *Hansard*, 2002, March 26, Column WA35).

A second example of the lack of cross-flow of information between the policing networks is found when fraud victimization surveys are compared with Internet-related frauds reported to the police. As was the case with computer security breaches, the surveys revealed high levels of victimization. In their 2000 survey Experian, for example, found that 57 per cent of all UK businesses had been victimized by fraudsters during the previous year. As with the study of security breaches, very few of the cases were reported to the police. Empirical research using police force databases found that only 120–150 Internet-related frauds per 1 million recorded crimes had been reported to the police and these were reasonably minor frauds. When extrapolated this represents about 1500 per year in all England and Wales.

What these disparities suggest is that each of the policing networks tends to have a different policing mandates relating to the protection of their specific set of interests, which seeks specific combinations of public and private models of justice outcomes. The relatively low levels of prosecutions for breaches of computer security and low levels of recorded Internet-related fraud are poignant illustrations of this conflict. In the former case, most breaches are dealt with by the victim organizations and in the latter, the issuing banks resolve most Internet-related frauds as part of their 'billing disputes' process. Both examples highlight the preference of corporate victims for private justice solutions instead of invoking public criminal justice processes that might expose their weaknesses to their commercial competitors (Wall, 2001, p. 174). They also show that each network tends to generate its own specific data, resulting in a number of reports and surveys that purport to estimate the extent of cybercrime, particularly with regard to cracking/hacking and commercial crime. Consequently, there can be up to five competing versions of the events relating to cybercrimes or harmful behaviour on the Internet and these multiple information flows have some profound implications for the production of knowledge about cybercrimes. Most notably, the lack of any form of officially recorded statistical instrument that informs policy makers of the size and scope of cybercrimes.

Media sensitisation

The Internet is so newsworthy a subject that a single dramatic case can shape public opinion and feed public anxiety (Grabosky & Smith, 1998), frequently resulting in demands for 'instant' solutions to what are extremely complex situations. Once created, these demands simply cannot be ignored, precisely because of the widespread fear of the consequences that they generate. There does not yet exist a recognized body of understanding to respond to public demand and inform policy because of the absence of 'reliable data'. Yet, the overall pervasiveness of the Internet medium, due to its ability to reach instantaneously such a massive audience and facilitate distributed interactions amongst it, raises questions as to whether 'reliable data' about cybercrimes could actually be created in the same way as for traditional crime.

Because of its aforementioned newsworthiness, media accounts of cybercrimes frequently invoke dramatic imagery of a helpless society being brought to its knees by an 'Electronic Pearl Harbour' (Smith, 1998; Taylor, 2001, p. 69) or a 'Cyber-Tsunami' (Wall, 2001, p. 2) and serve to sustain levels of public anxiety. Media sensitization, coupled with a corresponding lack of public knowledge about cybercrime, is gradually manipulating the legal and regulatory responses to harms by moulding public expectations, therefore providing regulatory bodies with a mandate (often implied) for taking action. Moreover, in the absence of any systematic calculation of the actual risk of cybercrimes, public anxiety is further heightened by the common failure of journalists, pressure groups and policy makers – also some academics – to discern between 'potential' and 'actual' harms. Once risk assessments are confused with reality (see Wall, 2001; Levi, 2001), the only perceived way to combat cybercrime is to use hard law and stringent technological countermeasures. This tends to shift the debate towards the needs of the state and corporate interests and away from important principles such as liberty and freedom of expression.

Online frauds provide an interesting example of the way that public knowledge can be shaped by news accounts that cite the findings of commercially produced surveys. Many of these surveys, see for example Experian's various retail fraud surveys, are conducted with methodological rigour to draw findings that indicate considerable increases in, and high levels of, online frauds. Such reports subsequently fuel sensational news stories which depict the Internet as an ungovernable space in which hapless users await victimization. But further analysis of these sources finds that they focus upon specific client/user groups, in this case, online retail outlets, and not individuals, yet the news media tend to generalize them. In fact with regard to online frauds, APACS (Association for Payment Clearing Services) statistics, subsequently verified by research (Wall, 2002b), indicate that the Internet is very secure for online transactions – as indicated earlier. Furthermore, the online retailers would expect some increase in their operational risks from fraud as they move their businesses from the high street to an online environment.

These increased operational risks are offset against the savings that retail operations make in terms of rental costs and also losses to merchandise through store-theft and in-store damage.

Shaping definitions of cybercrime

The tension that arises from the power struggle for control over cyberspace actively shapes definitions of 'good' and 'bad' behaviour. The increasing political and commercial power of the Internet encourages a new political economy of information capital and the forging of a new set of power relationships. Consequently, definitions of acceptable and unacceptable cyber-behaviour are themselves shaped by this ongoing power play, or 'intellectual land grab', that is currently taking place for (market) control (see Boyle, 1996). Of great concern is the increasing level of intolerance that is now being demonstrated by 'the new powerful', dominant groups that have emerged out of the power struggle, towards certain 'risk groups' that they perceive as a threat to their interests. A very practical example of this intolerance is reflected in the magnitude of the reaction by the music industry to the peer-to-peer Internet sites such as Gnutella and Napster (until recently), which distribute MP3 music files (see Carey & Wall, 2001, p. 36). Although intolerance tends to mould broader definitions of deviance, it would be wrong to assume that the construction of deviance is merely one-sided. Definitions of crime and deviance arise not only from the social activity of elites or powerful groups, but also from understandings of ordinary members of society as well as offenders themselves. As Melossi notes: 'the struggle around the definition of crime and deviance is located within the field of action that is constituted by plural and even conflicting efforts at producing control' (1994, p. 205).

CONCLUSIONS: CYBERCRIMES AND
THE NEW POLITICS OF SURVEILLANCE

This chapter has demonstrated that cybercrimes do not display characteristics that are common to models of understanding based upon traditional criminal behaviours, rather, they require new models of understanding. But problematic to developing such an understanding are a range of impediments to the systematic production of information about cybercrimes and the construction of 'reliable data' that policy makers recognize in order to inform their decision making. Indeed the asymmetric nature of cybercrime and the distributed environment in which it thrives probably renders impossible any attempts to obtain a full overview of victimization levels, because information about reported victimization does not flow through a single portal such as the police in the same way as does the reporting of traditional crimes. Perhaps the Internet questions in the forthcoming British Crime Surveys may illuminate the victimization issue when they are analysed.

What this chapter has also begun to explore is the growth in information capital arising from the shift in value from tangible to intangible forms; from physical objects to the virtual means by which ideas are expressed. It is therefore not surprising that offenders should manipulate and exploit multi-directional information flows over the Internet to capture information in order to exploit its value. So, there is a tension between the need to share information in order to participate on the Internet and the need to maintain the individual's right of control of his or her most private information. Yet, rather ironically, participants in online activities display a marked willingness to effectively forgo their privacy rights in return for a material, or informational, advantage to themselves (see Haggerty & Ericson, 2000; Poster, 1995). The reification of the privacy right from a moral right into a tradeable commodity is a process that is central to the new politics of surveillance. If the commodification of information is taken one step further, then lodged within the 'super-panopticon' of information databases (Poster, 1995) that contain our most private information is a goldmine of valuable data which can be mined using the tools of the new surveillance to illegitimate ends. Most topical at the time of writing is the example of Inland Revenue employees data mining the tax returns of celebrities for subsequent sale to the highest bidder, typically the media. For the media this prize information achieves the double whammy of creating stories that reveal the intimate secrets of celebrities, whilst also informing stories that expose the very weaknesses in the system that they, the media, sought initially to exploit. There is clearly a need for sensitive handling of personal information to prevent it being used for exploitative purposes.

Finally, in July 1993, cartoonist Peter Steiner published in the *New Yorker* a cartoon of two dogs watching a computer, which carried the caption: 'On the internet no one knows that you're a dog' (Vol. 69, No. 20, p. 61) which came to symbolize the mythical qualities of cyberspace. A decade later, the synoptic reality of this myth is that not only is there data out there to show others that you are a dog, but that same data will also tell them what colour fur you have!

8
The Constant State of Emergency?: Surveillance after 9/11

David Wood, Eli Konvitz and Kirstie Ball

In a piece of hyper techno-optimism in the conservative *City Journal*, Huber and Mills (2002) call for the extension of the dense urban infrastructure of automated software systems. 'Dispersed along roadsides, hills, and trails, they [micro-sensors] will report just about anything that may interest us – the passage of vehicles, the odor of explosives, the conversations of pedestrians, the look, sound, weight, temperature, even the smell, of almost anything.' In the climate of the US government's 'Terrorism Information Awareness' (TIA) campaign,[1] as pundits look forward to the increased reach of surveillance, this book has highlighted four important trends.

First, an intensification of local and everyday surveillance, but with an emphasis on the problematic nature of grand-scale developments. Second, the tendency of surveillance not only to 'creep' (Marx, 1995) forward but also to 'surge' at opportune moments, and new possibilities for the hindrance of its spread. Third, an interesting twist in the linkage between military and managerial surveillance activities, and fourth, a need for theory to take account of its practical complexities. This chapter examines each of these issues in turn.

THE INTENSIFICATION OF LOCAL AND EVERYDAY SURVEILLANCE

We set out the agenda for this collection by highlighting that the events of 9/11 accelerated trends and integrated various forces towards an intensification of surveillance in the Western world. We argued that the current situation has been progressively emerging throughout the twentieth century, with 9/11 being only one of a series of recent events that focus attention on surveillance as both a solution and the problem. In the preceding chapters, surveillance applications in areas of deviancy and security management, business practice, and law enforcement were examined. New occupational groups, technologies and organizations, from the public and private sector, and especially the media, have become more closely aligned under rubrics concerning national security, profits, and risk management, to intensify surveillance practice. At the same time conflicts and inconsistencies, and new possibilities for resistance, have also emerged.

Oscar Gandy, in his examination of data mining, highlighted the ease with which data are now stored and searched via sophisticated statistical techniques, at low costs. The statistician now becomes an agent of surveillance, as has the new generation of data mining software products, which compete and diffuse via the market. The same applies to digital cameras whose images can also be mined. The mainstream application of data-mining results in consumers' buying behaviour being more stringently defined, and the most value-added and risk-free customers being 'cherry picked' for the marketing of premium products. A more detailed category of person is being included and excluded from various domains of consumption.

Furthermore, companies that sell data mining technologies were some of the first to respond to the US government's appeal to find information about suspected terrorists. Modelling events based on the movements and transactions of suspected groups has become commonplace for data miners who use these tools in risk analysis and accident investigation. Given the integration of these technologies into a national security network, Gandy observes the significant privacy and human rights concerns that are associated with the virtual, rather than spatial, delineation of people, removing any strong basis of protest. Data mining, it seems, both extends and intensifies surveillance networks, and with privacy laws in his view having limited effect, mass media opinion, according to Gandy, is required to combat its spread.

Yet all is not lost. When *Charles Raab* examined problems with the leveraging of privacy codes to protect widespread abuse of personal information in the context of UK government, a fragmented picture emerged. To improve public services in the UK, public and private sector organizations have become more closely aligned, under a strategy called 'Information Age Government' (IAG) and are frequently reliant upon information technologies and data exchange to achieve this integration. With the immense potential for intensified surveillance of individual citizens via data-sharing, Raab questioned whether this alignment had been achieved in the first place, and examined the content and consistency of approaches to privacy used to protect personal data. Raab identified a 'ladder' of privacy concepts applied across different governmental organizations. The problem for IAG, but the reprieve for the privacy activist, is that the differentiated nature of governmental organizations means that information-sharing is difficult to achieve, despite IAG's wholistic rubric. Illustrations from the National Criminal Intelligence Service (NCIS) and the application of the Crime and Disorder Act show that the corollary (and downside) is that no unified approach to privacy is adopted either.

Privacy, it seems, is not an option for some offenders. In a climate where people's babies, pets and property are electronically tagged, *Mike Nellis* examined the troubled rise of the electronic monitoring of offenders, as used by the English probation service. Still vociferously opposed by the Howard League, electronic monitoring (EM), or 'tagging', emerged as a new form of community control in the 1990s, allowing prisoners to be released early from their sentences, and enabling non-custodial sentences for young offenders. As with any new surveillance technology, EM caused the alignment of new organizations and actors, in this case outside the traditional boundaries of the probation service, in its development and application. Private security companies who make the product, new monitoring staff (who incidentally, lacked the traditional social work or probationary skills), as well as the probation service and its work culture, were involved. Significant testing of its effects involved probation services and organizations from Scotland and the US. As a surveillance technique, it still courts controversy from those who say that it isn't a severe enough punishment, equating its tracking ability to the more common-place technologies found in mobile phones and pagers. It is significantly different from these, however, achieving remote control in real time via offender's bodies, and using data mining techniques to identify those offenders most suitable to be tagged. Even though this potentially powerful and intense surveillance technology has its shortcomings, Nellis argued that it paves the way for more exacting developments in electronic offender management.

The media, as an important vehicle for messages about the legitimacy or otherwise of surveillance practice, was discussed in all of the early chapters. Then, *Frank Webster* and *David Wall* highlighted the central role played by the media in modern forms of information warfare, and in policing and enabling crime on the Internet.

Frank Webster examined the integral part the media play in modern wars, both as an agent of surveillance and as a body whose messages are themselves monitored by participating states. Adopting a broad definition of media to include everything from newspapers to the Internet, Webster observed that because of the rise of information, rather than industrial, warfare, what gets reported, and the manner of the reportage may now alter the course of military action. Frequently described as 'the eyes of the world', the media are clearly implicated in surveillance networks, both intensifying it through their activity, and promoting resistance to it through debate. Forms of media, and individual journalists, are caught in an awkward position in the practice of surveillance, simultaneously acting in a panoptic and synoptic capacity. Moreover, the practical and moral difficulties associated with controlling the media, and their inherent interest in covering the drama of international conflict, ensure that the media are a vital group to include if both public and national interests are to be served in the coverage and process of war.

Similarly *David Wall* also drew upon panoptic and synoptic notions to describe the Internet as media through which 'traditional' crimes are perpetrated more efficiently, and new forms of crime have emerged. The range of cybercrimes is now so large in terms of impact, not only are the police, and other enforcement agencies drawing upon tools of surveillance (e.g. data mining) to combat these crimes, the criminals themselves are also using the same tools to enable their perpetration. The mass media are also involved in this assemblage. In spite of the fact that they have chosen to focus on a small range of very high-profile, hideous offences, such as child pornography and paedophile rings, the everyday practice of spamming, based on data mining techniques, is a cybercrime of which we are all victims as regular Internet users. Surveillance techniques creep into everyday usage by criminal, as well as governmental agencies.

So, in the current climate, private security firms, government agencies and armed forces, media organizations, statisticians, journalists, probation officers, and criminals are now more closely involved in surveillance practices. Legislation, government policy and media cultures carry messages of hope and despair in their wakes. But what of this alignment and spread of surveillance? How are we to understand, particularly in the light of TIA, the drivers and restrainers of surveillance?

SURVEILLANCE 'CREEP', 'SURGE' AND THE REVERSE SALIENT

Gary Marx argued that surveillance technologies, techniques and processes are extended by a gradual 'surveillance creep' (Marx, 1995), wherein new uses are found for existing technologies and rationales found for expansion in subtle ways that avoid public attention. The spread of surveillance, however, is not always a gradual one. Sometimes there are periods of 'surveillance surge', often sparked by particular events, like 9/11 or the murder of Jamie Bulger in the UK in the early 1990s (Norris & Armstrong, 1999). Referred to by Innes (2001) as 'trigger crimes', these events allow the rapid and overt introduction of new technologies with less public debate than usual, because they are perceived as necessary responses to a changed situation. The most important thing to note about events like 9/11 in terms of surveillance is that they legitimate existing trends, inventions and legislation and allow their extension in ways that were often not intended, and which may be ineffective.

It is thus not simply a case that these events spark what Gandy calls 'a Schumpeterian swarm of innovation'. Though innovation is prompted by such events, the immediate reaction, the initial surveillance surge, consists of those with already developed technologies to promote and sell, taking advantage of crises or emotional moments in the public consciousness to push their product as a solution, however spurious, to the crisis. To take two examples: in the UK, the Home Office is planning an 'entitlement card' for all those wishing to claim state benefits, starting with asylum seekers, who are in the least position to object. The European Union's ID plans too are posited on a database of refugees and asylum seekers' fingerprints and facial profiles. In addition, many airports are now offering biometric check-ins for regular business class passengers. Both solutions have been promoted using post-9/11 rhetoric, yet it is quite clear that neither biometric ID for refugees and asylum seekers nor airport fast-track iris-scanning for frequent fliers would have had any impact on the events of 9/11 (or indeed would on any similar future incidents). In both cases, the implementation of tools to compensate for inefficiencies in the existing infrastructures, picking up at the same time on opportunities for 'cherry-picking' and splintering, created new efficiencies in surveillance as knock-on effects, and had little to do with plans for the prevention of terrorism. They have, in fact, far more to do with existing trends towards the intensification of categorization and exclusion on a global scale, which, it could be argued, *contributes* to reactionary violence and terrorism.

Instead of dealing with the extraordinary, periods of surveillance surge instead allow the further ordering of everyday life, what Nellis calls the 'extension of managerial culture'. Software-driven systems are allowing further industrialization of everyday life through what appears to be a combination of the physical and virtual, leading to both spatial (territorial) and analytical (information-based) exclusion (Thrift & French, 2002). This can also be considered an aspect of what Norris, adapting Lianos and Douglas (2000), calls 'Automated Socio-Technical Environments' (ASTEs), systems that at the same time facilitate those with the correct credentials and exclude others (Norris, 2002) using data mining techniques. Almost everything is now code, or as Nellis puts it, everything has the potential to be digitally tagged.

Indeed, Raab's, Gandy's, and Nellis's discussions are reflected in American proposals and policy for airport security. The US Transportation Security Administration (TSA) confirmed in November 2002 that a list exists that bars access to flights for those who have been named 'threats to aviation' (Lindorff, 2002). This list, comprising around 1000 names, is sometimes accompanied by another list of lower-risk individuals who should be watched closely but are not necessarily to be prevented from flying. The information in one system will, according to one source (O'Harrow, 2002), include seven layers of passenger associates, taking rather literally the now-popular notion (after Stanley Milgram's famous 1967 experiment) that any two people can be connected with a chain of 'six degrees of separation'. These people have no recourse; because the TSA simply compiles lists of high-risk individuals from other federal agencies, it is not responsible for the actual content of the final list. The FBI, CIA and other source agencies are the only entities that know why a particular name is on that list, even if there has been a mistake.

In addition to the no-fly list, a system for screening of airline passengers called Computer Assisted Passenger Pre-Screening (CAPPS) already existed before 9/11. It looks at factors such as a person's travel history, the type of ticket (one-way or round-trip?) and how it was paid for (cash or credit card?). Unfortunately, it did not prevent the terrorists boarding planes: they had all tested the system by flying to see whether they would be denied boarding passes. Nine of the 9/11 hijackers were subjected to extra scrutiny, but all were cleared. In efforts to prevent that happening again, systems are now being developed that make both the simple list as well as CAPPS seem rudimentary.

Some of the newest potential technologies seem implausible, for example 'Brain Fingerprinting'[2] (Greene, 2001) or 'Smart Dust'[3] (Economist, 2002). NASA has already created a system that alerts pilots or astronauts when they stop concentrating; NASA's current goal (Murray, 2002) is to measure the brainwaves and heartbeats of passengers as they pass through security screening and to compare the data with that of 'normal' individuals.

Nevertheless, the experience of 9/11 suggests that these seemingly impenetrable systems can fail. Could it be that the authorities have overestimated the technical capability of the systems? Work by Hughes (1983) on electricity networks, suggests that this can sometimes be attributed to another phenomenon, which works hand in hand with the surveillance 'surge'. Hughes used the idea of a 'reverse salient' to describe a situation in which an expanding system is slowed by one or more components or parts that do not perform on a par with the rest of the system. In the early and mid-1990s, for example, British visual surveillance systems were held back by slow network growth and a lack of training and operational guidelines for operators. By the late 1990s, most city-centre systems' networks were already in place and standards organizations had made concerted efforts to develop codes of practice. As networks continued to expand, they reached the limits of the older analogue technology. Videotapes became cumbersome and difficult to track, manage and search; large systems required ever-larger switching equipment. The very format of the signals had become a reverse salient, and manufacturers and installers began to shift from analogue to digital data-transmission and capture systems. New post-9/11 initiatives aimed at connecting various surveillance and dataveillance systems will no doubt find several reverse salients that hinder their progress.

THE MILITARY AND THE MANAGERIAL

A common theme of the chapters was the increasing crossover between the military and management. Whilst this is not new in surveillance studies (Bogard, 1996; Giddens, 1985; Dandeker, 1990), the direction of this cross-fertilization is. Whilst it's generally taken as read that the widespread diffusion of surveillance technologies such as CCTV began with military innovation and then spread to the business enterprise, it is clear from many of the chapters in this book that governments and their military arms are now turning to software houses and technologists for more sophisticated tools to track and pre-empt crime and terror. As the two domains constantly redefine their relationship, this trend is something that is characteristic of our times.

According to Bauman (1995, p. 193), the twentieth century was characterized by fast and efficient killing, scientifically designed and administered genocide. Ponting (1999) argues in *Progress and Barbarism* that modernity consists of a seemingly inescapable dialectical relationship: striving towards better social conditions while at the same time, horribly uncivil, violent and regressive episodes show no sign of declining as the twenty-first century begins. The casual ease with which wars are reported as entertainment, the consensus between major political parties about the support for military operations, and the continued growth of military surveillance systems themselves, also support the case that the military enjoys a huge degree of – largely unspoken, unnoticed and uncontested – support.

This is partly a matter of discourse, a militarization of language and social concepts. State and mass media talk of 'threat assessment', the 'war on drugs', the 'war on crime', of toughness in the law, of 'zero tolerance', and so on. 'Information warfare' has come out of the dark shadows of military covert operations and into the bright light of the business world, where corporate espionage is rife and the computer penetration and security specialists are redesignated as 'knowledge warriors'. But is this reflected in the material reality of products or organizational structures, or is it merely an example of business leaders reading too much Sun-Tzu and macho mid-life fantasies of playing soldiers?

Much as it is an incomplete process, military surveillance is also one of the few phenomena that can be argued to be truly global in an age where everything is supposedly being globalized. De Landa (1991) describes this further extension of panopticism beyond the visual into the whole electromagnetic spectrum, as a Panspectron. Transnational communications systems are thoroughly interpenetrated and infiltrated by military surveillance systems: even their invention, design and protocols have military elements. One example is the Internet. This transnational system of network connections and protocols was in no small part based on the American military's ARPANET distributed communications system, designed to survive destruction of particular parts of the system (Rheingold, 1993). The entire history of modern computing from its origins and through its early development is based in World War II and cold war systems, the aim being the creation of the planet as a 'closed world', a totally defensible and secure space (Edwards, 1996; de Landa, 1991).

The business of major arms manufacturers has also shifted towards mainstream security and surveillance products. TRW, a major part of the US defence firmament, is also a leader in civilian biometrics; in the UK, QinetiQ, the semi-privatized company, was formerly known as the Defence Evaluation and Research Agency (DERA); and Sagem, in France, manufactures everything from mobile phones through surveillance algorithms to unmanned aerial reconnaissance systems. There is growing evidence of a shift amongst military supply and arms companies towards the civilian market, and in some cases creating new markets for innovative products that are no longer purely military or civilian (Wright, 1998; Doucet & Lloyd, 2001). Examples of these crossover products include less-lethal and non-lethal weaponry and, with particular relevance to surveillance, killing and paralysing systems linked to surveillance cameras, and cashpoints that are able to physically detain a person who consistently enters the wrong PIN number. Clearly, such systems will not appear on our high streets tomorrow, nor will one find their makers exhibiting at conventional security equipment fairs. They remain a highly specialized and specialist market.

Surveillance creep suggests that activists should remain vigilant of these developments. Many argued that evidence of arms manufacturers shifting into civilian production represented a positive trend, the civilianization of the military-industrial complex; as a part of the 'peace dividend', social benefits would supposedly flow from detente and represented progress to 'post-military society' (Shaw, 1991). Manufacturers who previously specialized in military contracting have moved into civilian production, but without abandoning their military roots entirely. Industry is far more aware that war generates profits than were the hopeful, perhaps naive, post-cold war advocates of a generalized 'peace dividend'. Instead of a more peaceful civil society and international situation, states, following the US, have reorientated the definition of threat from large global enemies with 'fifth column' allies to the disaffected and deprived at both national and international level. Within nations, police and urban planners are returning to Victorian notions of the 'threat' from dangerous classes of people, instead of the previously dominant conception of criminality as individual 'deviancy' from social norms. The trend is continuing after 9/11, the populations of several Western countries being told that they should be prepared for a constant state of emergency, as the American 'war on terrorism' would imply. Cross-fertilization between the military and the managerial is clearly central to problems and developments in the study and practice of surveillance and should not be ignored by analysts or activists.

THE SCALE(-ING) OF THE PROBLEM

This final, and most important point for surveillance theorists in particular, highlighted in this book, is the scale and complexity of surveillance practice. Both UK and US governments have huge ambitions concerning the integration of personal information of the population, electronically integrated government, and slick, blood-free (on their part), information-intense warfare. Despite this, the chapters have highlighted the tensions and conflicts, not just at the very local level, but also the organizational, inter-organizational, and inter-state levels of surveillance practice.

The level at which we study surveillance will, for a large part, determine, and maybe even narrow research findings. For example, seen from the transnational scale, American military surveillance seems the predominant force even after 9/11. It appears involved in a dynamic web of relationships with both the operation of neo-liberal capitalism and the Western democratic social model, and with the panoptic impulses of the dominant transnational class. The global Panspectron, of which military satellites and space weapons are only a small part, is concerned with monitoring behaviour at all levels from the individual in real and virtual space, to groups and to states in global politics and economics. Politically deviant countries can be identified as 'rogue states'; neo-liberal economic institutions like the IMF have for some time been identifying economically deviant states, monitoring their compliance with international norms and if necessary enforcing structural adjustment of their economies (Gill, 1995). Surveillance is involved in a complex iterative relationship both with the mode of production and with violence.

However, in Newham (London, UK), American military surveillance seems very distant, and the idea of a single encircling and omniscient, indeed competent, surveillant structure seems faintly ridiculous. Identix (formerly Visionics) is the leading manufacturer of facial recognition technologies, and, with installer Dectel, is piloting its FaceIT system in the borough of Newham. This has attracted widespread media coverage and opposing claims. Left-leaning London newspaper the *Guardian* featured an experiment by one of its reporters, James Meek, in which he had his facial profile placed in the Newham database, and then wandered around Newham to see whether he would be detected (Meek, 2002). He claimed that the system did not recognize him once, adding to suspicions about it. Previous studies have shown that there has not been a single arrest associated with the pilot project and local police spokespeople have fallen back on the deterrence argument to justify its effectiveness. When pressed, the Managing Director of Dectel was quick to point out that apart from the software, the system's hit rate also depends upon, first, cameras spotting the right suspect in the first place, and second, adequate maintenance and operation of the hardware, not just the software.[4] Eventually admitting that some of the algorithms may actually be problematic, its budget has apparently since been reduced drastically, and there is less enthusiasm for it. Similar concerns were voiced about the reports of ACLU into FaceIT in use in Tampa Bay, Florida, in which no verifiable success was recorded (Stanley & Steinhardt, 2002). For technologists at the September 2002 UK Police Information Technology Organisation (PITO) seminar,[5] this experiment was still considered considerable progress, in contrast to ACLU, who saw it as a potentially dangerous technology in terms of human rights. The engineering view is markedly different from that of the campaigner, and corporate power is only one factor in a complex story that involved policing, the UK state, local government, private sector security, the critique of human rights campaigners and the relationship between large US producers of facial recognition software and small UK systems manufacturers. In the case of Newham, one can see the gradual deterioration of a system that was already problematic in its basic encoding, to a point where the application becomes more a matter of placing it within a growing mythology of CCTV.

There is indeed a complex series of movements at work. This iterative process manifests itself not only in the new technological components of surveillance (computers, surveillance equipment), but also in the conceptual architecture of control: the movement from deviance to dangerization (Lianos & Douglas, 2000), or the notion of problematic objects (Bloomfield, 2001); the return to ideas of pre-emption (Marx, 2002), prediction (Gandy, Nellis, this volume) and predetermined character (Rose, 2000); the physical splintering of urban spaces into closed and defensible enclaves, communication and transport corridors (Graham & Marvin, 2001); and the militarization of policing, borders and cities. The onward spread of surveillance does not derive from a purely civil logic (whether economic or social) as those authors seem to indicate; rather, both the technologies and the processes are derived from a complex interaction between military and economic logics. The process of militarization of everyday life is hidden both because of a belief, largely unsupported by evidence, in the ideas of post-military society and liberal democratic peace (a belief which is being reinforced even as terrorism and the 'war on terrorism' continue their escalatory activities worldwide), and because of the emergent nature of change in complex socio-technical systems.

The complex interweaving processes that take place between the social and the technical, and the civil and the military, need to be far better theorized. This is particularly important if one is to take seriously Gary Marx's 'new surveillance' argument (Marx, 2002), and the assertion that it is technologies, particularly information technology, that have made the surveillance society possible. While surveillance has long been acknowledged to work in a network-like fashion (Foucault, 1979) few recent studies of surveillance have addressed it, either empirically or theoretically, in this fashion (Ball, 2002). In the context of modern, digital surveillance, the software development suites facilitate panopticism; scientists, engineers and programmers are involved in state, military and corporate networks and are key parts in the development and functioning of surveillance systems. These people make the decisions that affect the invisible programming of the systems in the market place; elsewhere, another individual reasoned that a fit of so many pixels was enough to identify a face in a biometric system. These invisible, but influential decisions, their influence, and diffusion are poorly documented in the surveillance literature.

In conclusion, we would urge readers who are studying, planning to study, or thinking about surveillance practice to responsibly consult and apply the multitude of social-theoretical tools at their disposal. Social Worlds Theory (Bowker & Star, 1999) and Communities of Practice (Brown & Duguid, 2000) attempt to reposition social theory as a theory of movement and process (for example Harvey, 1996; Urry, 2000), and newly reviewed theories of the subject (Boyne, 2000) would all be beneficial in creating an understanding of the growth, spread and intensification of surveillance. Research should attempt to take the experiences of watched consumer, software developer, and the gated community into account, as well as the interests of organizations and states in protecting their interests, rather than their citizens, using surveillance-based techniques.

Surveillance is a uniquely simple concept, but is an empirically complex, emergent phenomenon, and is inextricably bound up with issues of power. Its growth, operation and effectiveness are continually evolving. With the presence of Total Information Awareness, it is important for students, researchers and activists to be reflexive on the findings, meanings and understandings of surveillance that they create. It would be foolish to try to ascribe a single origin in any place or event to account for the intensification of surveillance. But with governments and capital having so much to gain from its success, it will pay for the rest of us to be vigilant.

NOTES

1. See http://www.darpa.mil/iao/TIASystems.htm for further details.
2. Brainwave Science Web site: http://www.brainwavescience.com
3. 'SMART DUST: Autonomous sensing and communication in a cubic millimetre'. University of California at Berkeley Robotics Laboratory. http://robotics.eeecs.Berkeley.edu/~pister/Smartdust/
4. Conversation with John Ellis, MD Dectel, September 9, 2002.
5. Biometrics and Law Enforcement, September 9, 2002, Department of Trade Conference Centre, London, UK.

Notes on Contributors

Kirstie Ball is Lecturer in Organizational Management, Department of Commerce, University of Birmingham. She is the author of a number of theoretical and empirical papers on surveillance in organizations, and is joint editor of *Surveillance and Society*, a new electronic journal dedicated to surveillance studies. She has spoken nationally and internationally on surveillance at work, and has spoken in the UK national media on the issue.

Oscar H. Gandy is Professor at the Annenberg School for Communication, University of Pennsylvania. His research interests include privacy and communication in the information society, social participation and racial identity. His most recent books include *Framing Public Life* (edited with Stephen Reese and August Grant, Lawrence Erlbaum, 2001) and *Communication and Race: A Structural Perspective* (Edward Arnold and Oxford University Press, 1998). He has also published in the *Journal of Social Issues, Journal of Business Ethics* and *Journal of Black Studies*.

Eli Konvitz earned a BA in History from the Johns Hopkins University, and is pursuing a PhD in the School of Architecture, Planning and Landscape at the University of Newcastle upon Tyne. Combining personal interests in systems and networks, in privacy and the relationship of the individual to society, and in cities and urbanism, he is studying the geographical development of closed-circuit television surveillance in the UK.

David Lyon is Professor of Sociology at Queens University, Kingston, Canada. His research interests include the sociology of communication and information technologies; surveillance and privacy; cyberspace; post/modernity; contemporary religion; sociology and christianity; and social theory. His recent publications include: *Surveillance Society: Monitoring Everyday Life* (Open University Press, 2001), *Surveillance as Social Sorting* (Routledge, 2002) and *Jesus in Disneyland: Religion in Postmodern Times* (Polity Press/Blackwell, 2000).

Mike Nellis is Senior Lecturer in Criminal Justice at the University of Birmingham. His research focuses upon areas of penal policy, the probation service, crime prevention, drugs, youth justice work and voluntary organisations in the criminal justice system. He has published in the *Howard Journal of Criminal Justice*, the *British Journal of Criminology* and the *Prison Service Journal*.

Charles D. Raab is Professor of Government at the University of Edinburgh. His main research interests are in public policy and governance, including British government, education policy, information policy (privacy protection and public access to information) and information technology in democratic politics, government and commerce. Publications include *Governing Education: A Sociology of Policy Since 1945* (with A. McPherson, Edinburgh University Press, 1988); *Policing the European Union* (with M. Anderson et al., Clarendon Press, 1995); *The Governance of Schooling: Comparative Studies of Devolved Management* (with M. Arnott, ed., Routledge/Falmer, 2000), and many contributions to journals and edited volumes.

David S. Wall is Senior Lecturer in Criminology at the University of Leeds. His research interests include Policing, Access to Criminal Justice, Law and Popular Culture, Sociology of Law, Information Technology, Cybercrimes, Cyberlaw, and the Legal Regulation of Knowledge. Some of his recent publications include *Cyberspace Crime* (Ashgate/Dartmouth, 2002); *Crime and the Internet* (Routledge, 2001); *Policy Networks in Criminal Justice* (with Mick Ryan and Steve Savage, Palgrave/Macmillan Press, 2001); and *The Internet, Law and Society* (ed. with Clive Walker and Yaman Akdeniz, Longman, 2000).

Frank Webster is Professor of Sociology at City University, London. He is author and editor/co-editor most recently of *Culture and Politics in the Information Age* (Routledge, 2001), *The Virtual University?* (Oxford University Press, 2002), *The Information Society Reader* (Routledge, 2003) and *Manuel Castells* (3 vols) (Sage, 2004). He is currently working on *Information and Uncertainty: Living with 21st Century Capitalism*.

David Wood Dr David Wood is Earl Grey Postdoctoral Research Fellow at the University of Newcastle's School of Architecture Planning and Landscape. His current project looks at the socio-technical history and development of computer-mediated surveillance technologies. His other research interests include: geographies of military intelligence and orbital space; virtual spaces; the militarization of the city; and social theory. He is also Managing Editor of the international journal of surveillance studies, *Surveillance and Society*, www.surveillance-and-society.org.

Bibliography

Abrams, P. (1982) *Historical Sociology* (Shepton Mallet: Open Books)

Agreement between The Attorneys General of the States of Arizona, California, Connecticut, Massachusetts, Michigan, New Jersey, New Mexico, New York, Vermont and Washington and DoubleClick, Inc. (2002), August 26

Allchin, W. (1989) Chaperones, Escorts, Trackers, Taggers. *Friend*, June 30

Allen-Bell, A. (1997) The Birth of the Crime 'Driving While Black' (DWB). *Southern University Law Review* Vol. 25

American Civil Liberties Union (ACLU) (2002) Drawing a Blank: Tampa Police Records Reveal Poor Performance of Face-Recognition Technology. *Press Release*, January 3 <http://www.aclu.org/Privacy/Privacy.cfm?ID=10210&c=39>

Anderson, M., den Boer, M., Cullen, P., Gilmore, W., Raab, C. and Walker, N. (1995) *Policing the European Union* (Oxford: Clarendon Press)

Anthony, P. and Margroff, R.E. (1986 [1968]) *The Ring* (New York: Tom Doherty Associates)

APACS (2002) *Card Fraud: The Facts* (London: Association of Payment and Clearing Services)

Arquilla, J. and Ronfeldt, D.F. (eds) (1997) *In Athena's Camp: Preparing for Conflict in the Information Age* (Santa Monica, CA: RAND)

Aungles, A. (1994) *The Prison and the Home: A Study of the Relationship between Domesticity and Penalty* (Sydney: Institute of Criminology Monographs)

Ball, K. (2002) Elements of Surveillance: A New Framework and Future Research Directions. *Information, Communication and Society* Vol. 5 No. 4

Ball, R., Huff, R. and Lilly J.R. (1988) *House Arrest and Correctional Policy: Doing Time at Home* (Newbury Park, CA: Sage)

Bamford, J. (2001) *Body of Secrets: Anatomy of the Ultra-Secret National Security Agency* (New York: Doubleday)

Barber, B. (1995) *Jihad versus McWorld: How Globalism and Tribalism are Reshaping the World* (New York: Ballentine Books)

Barkham, J. (2001) Information Warfare and International Law on the Use of Force. *New York Journal of International Law and Politics* Vol. 34 No. 1

Barlow, J.P. (1994) The Economy of Ideas: A Framework for Rethinking Patents and Copyrights in the Digital Age (Everything You Know about Intellectual Property is Wrong). *Wired* Vol. 2 No. 3

Bateman, T. (2001) Custodial Sentencing of Children: Prospects for Reversing the Tide. *Youth Justice* Vol. 1 No. 1

Baudrillard, J. (1991) *La Guerre du Golfe n'a pas eu lieu* (Paris: Galilée)

Bauman, Z. (1987) *Modernity and the Holocaust* (Oxford: Blackwell)

—— (1995) *Life in Fragments: Essays in Postmodern Modernity* (Oxford: Blackwell)

—— (1997) *Postmodernity and Its Discontents* (Cambridge: Polity Press)

—— (2000) Social Uses of Law and Order. In D. Garland and R. Sparks (eds) *Criminology and Social Theory* (Oxford: Oxford University Press)

Baumer, T. and Mendelsohn, R. (1995) A Cautionary Tale about Electronically Monitored Home Detention. In K. Schulz (ed.) *Electronic Monitoring and Corrections: The Policy, the Operation, the Research* (Vancouver: Simon Fraser University)

Bellamy, C. and Taylor, J. (1998) *Governing in the Information Age* (Buckingham: Open University Press)

Bennett, C. and Raab, C. (2003) *The Governance of Privacy: Policy Instruments in Global Perspective* (Aldershot: Ashgate)

Bennett, W.L. and Paletz, D.L. (eds) (1994) *Taken by Storm: The Media, Public Opinion, and U.S. Foreign Policy in the Gulf War*, American Politics and Political Economy Series (Chicago: University of Chicago Press).

Berg, A. (1996) Playing Tag. *The Magistrate* Vol. 52, No. 5

Berkowitz, B. (2003) The New Face of War: *How War Will Be Fought in the 21st Century* (New York: Free Press)

Blair, A. (2001) *Speech to Labour Party Conference* (Brighton: Labour Party) October 2

Bloomfield B. (2001) In the Right Place at the Right Time: Electronic Tagging and Problems of Social Order/Disorder. *Sociological Review* Vol. 49 No. 2

Bobbitt, P. (2002) *The Shield of Achilles: War, Peace and the Course of History* (London: Allen Lane)

Bogard, William (1996) *The Simulation of Surveillance: Hypercontrol in Telematic Societies* (Cambridge: Cambridge University Press)

Bok, S. (1984) *Secrets: Concealment and Revelation* (Oxford: Oxford University Press)

Booker, C. (2002) European Traffic Control to be Based in Space. *Sunday Telegraph*, March 3

Bottoms, A.E., Gelsthorpe, L. and Rex, S. (eds) (2001) *Community Penalties: Change and Challenges* (Cullompton, Devon: Willan)

Bowker, G. and Star, S. (1999) *Sorting Things Out: Classification and Its Consequences* (Cambridge, MA: MIT Press)

Bowman, L. (2002) FBI Wants to Track Your Web Trail. *ZDNet News,* June 6 <zdnet.com.com/2100–1105–933202.html>

Boyle, J. (1996) *Shamans, Software and Spleens: Law and the Construction of the Information Society* (Cambridge, MA: Harvard University Press)

Boyne, R. (2000) Post-Panopticism. *Economy and Society* Vol. 29 No. 2

Braithwaite, J. (1992) *Crime, Shame and Reintegration* (Cambridge: Cambridge University Press)

Braverman, H. (1974) *Labour and Monopoly Capital: The Degradation of Work in the Twentieth Century* (New York: Monthly Review Press)

—— (1980) *Labour and Monopoly Capital* (New York: Monthly Review Press)

Brenner, S. (2001) Is There Such a Thing as 'Virtual Crime'? *California Criminal Law Review* Vol. 4 No. 1, also at <http://www.boalt.org/CCLR/v4/v4brenner.htm>

Brightmail (2002) *Slamming Spam* (San Francisco: Brightmail)

Brown, J.S. and Duguid P. (2000) *The Social Life of Information* (Boston, MA: HBR Books)

Brownlie, I. and Goodwin-Gill, G.S. (2002) *Basic Documents on Human Rights*, 4th edition (Oxford: Oxford University Press)

Burnham, D. (1983) *The Rise of the Computer State* (London: Weidenfeld and Nicolson)

Campbell, D. (1999) Trawler's Empty Net. *The Guardian Online*, June 24

Campbell, D. and Connor, S. (1986) *On the Record: Surveillance, Computers and Privacy* (London: Michael Joseph)

Cannings, J. (2002) A Walk around the Lake. *Vista: Perspectives on Probation* Vol. 7 No. 1

Carey, M. and Wall, D.S. (2001) MP3: More Beats to the Byte. *International Review of Law, Computers and Technology* Vol. 15.

Castells, M. (1996) *The Rise of the Network Society* (Oxford: Blackwell)

—— (1996–98) *The Information Age*, 3 volumes (Oxford: Blackwell)

Cavoukian, A. (1998, January) *Data Mining: Striking a Claim on your Privacy* (Ontario: Information and Privacy Commissioner)

Chatterjee, B. (2001) Last of the Rainmacs? Thinking about Pornography in Cyberspace. In D.S. Wall (ed.) *Crime and the Internet* (London: Routledge)

Chibnall, S. (1977) *Law and Order News: An Analysis of Crime Reporting in the British Press* (London: Tavistock)

Claire Cherry v. Amoco Oil Co., 490 *F.Supp.* 1026 (N.D. Ga. 1980)

Cohen, E.A. (1996) A Revolution in Warfare. *Foreign Affairs* Vol. 75 No. 2, March–April

Committee on Women's Imprisonment (2000) *Justice for Women* (London: Penal Reform Trust)

Compuserve (1997) *CompuServe Inc. v. Cyber Promotions, Inc. and Sanford Wallace*, 962 *F.Supp.* 1015 (S.D. Ohio Feb. 3, 1997)

Conquest, Robert (1971 [1968]), *The Great Terror: Stalin's Purge of the Thirties* (Harmondsworth: Penguin)

Crovitz, L. (2002) Info@FBI.gov. *The Wall Street Journal Online*, June 5 <online.wsj.com/article/0,,SB10232602495103600.djm,00.html>

Curtis, L. (1984) *Ireland: The Propaganda War* (London: Pluto Press)

Dandeker, C. (1990) *Surveillance, Power and Modernity* (Cambridge: Polity Press)

Danna, A. and Gandy, O. (2002) All That Glitters is Not Gold: Digging Beneath the Surface of Data Mining. *Journal of Business Ethics* Vol. 40

DARPA (Defence Advanced Research Projects Agency) (2002) *Mission Statement, Information Awareness Office* <http://www.afcea.org/pastevents/fallintel2002/DARPAPresentationfiles/side0154.htm

Darrow, B. (2002) Slamming Spam: Brightmail to Offer Antispam Services to Integrators, VARs. *Computer Reseller News*, August 23 <http://crn.channel-supersearch.com/news/crn/37067.asp>

Davies, S. (1996) *Big Brother: Britain's Web of Surveillance and the New Technological Order* (London: Pan)

De Landa, M. (1991) *War in the Age of Intelligent Machines* (New York: Zone)

Deleuze, G. and Guattari, F. (1987) *A Thousand Plateaus* (Minneapolis: University of Minneapolis Press)

Democracy Online Project (2002) Report. Privacy and Online Politics. Is Online Profiling Doing More Harm Than Good for Citizens in Our Political System? The George Washington University <dop@gwu.edu>

Dennis, S. (1999) 75% of Brits Happy to Give Firms their Personal Data. *YAHOO News Asia*, May 18

Dodgson, K., Goodwin, P., Howard, P. et al. (2001) *Electronic Monitoring of Released Prisoners: An Evaluation of the Home Detention Curfew Scheme. Home Office Research Study 222* (London: Home Office)

Doucet, I. and Lloyd R. (eds) (2001) *Alternative Anti-Personnel Mines: The Next Generation* (London/Berlin: Landmine Action/German Initiative to Ban Landmines)

Draper, H. (1971) *Private Police* (Harmondsworth: Penguin)

DTI (2002) *Information Security Breaches Survey 2002*, executive summary, <http://www.dti.gov.uk/cii/docs/sbsexecsum_2002.pdf>

Dunbar, I. and Langdon, A. (1998) *Tough Justice: Sentencing and Penal Policies in the 1990s* (London: Blackstone)

Economist (2002) Desirable Dust: How Smart Sensors Can Monitor the Real World, 362 (8258), Special Section 8–9

Edwards, L. (2000) Canning the Spam: Is There a Case For the Legal Control of Junk Electronic Mail? In L. Edwards and C. Wealde (eds) *Law and the Internet: A framework for Electronic Commerce*, 2nd edition (Oxford: Hart Publishing)

Edwards, P.N. (1996) *The Closed World: Computers and the Politics of Discourse in Cold War America* (Cambridge, MA: MIT Press)

Elegant, R. (1981) How to Lose a War. *Encounter* Vol. 57 No. 2, August

Elliot, R., Airs, J. and Webb, S. (1999) *Community Penalties for Fine Default and Persistent Petty Offending*. Research Findings No. 98 (London: Home Office)

Ellison, L. (nd) <http://www.siliconvalley.com/cgi-bin/>

Ellul, J. (1964) *The Technological Society* (New York: Vintage)

Engberg, D. (1996) The Virtual Panopticon. *Impact of New Media Technologies*, Fall <http://is.gseis.ucla.edu/impact/f96/Projects/dengberg/>

Ericson, R. and Haggerty, K. (1997) *Policing the Risk Society* (Toronto: University of Toronto Press)

EU Directive (2002) *EU Directive on Privacy and Electronic Communications* (2002/58/EC), July 12

European Parliament (2000) *Prison Technologies: An Appraisal of Technologies of Political Control*. Working document for the Scientific and Technological Options Assessment Panel of the European Parliament. Luxembourg

FBI Asks Libraries For Records of People Suspected of Terror Ties (2002). *The Wall Street Journal Online*, June 24 <online.wsj.com/article/0,,SB1024963982754360320.djm,00.html>

FBI/CSI (2002) *2002 Computer Crime and Security Survey*. <http://www.gocsi.com/pdfs/fbi/FBI2002.pdf>

Feeley, M. and Simon, J. (1994) Actuarial Justice: The Emerging New Criminal Law. In D. Nelken (ed.) *The Futures of Criminology* (London: Sage)

Fionda, J. (2000) New Managerialism, Credibility and the Sanitisation of Criminal Justice. In P. Green and A. Rutherford (eds) *Criminal Justice in Transition* (Oxford: Hart Publishing)

Fischer-Hubner, S. (2001) *IT-Security and Privacy: Design and Use of Privacy-Enhancing Security Mechanisms* (New York: Springer)

Fitzpatrick, R.C. (1967 [1965]) The Circuit Riders. In J.W. Campbell (ed.) *Analog Two* (London: Panther Books)

Fletcher, H. (2002) Home Detention Curfew – No Answer to Jail Crisis. *Napo News*, 137

Foucault, M. (1978) *A History of Sexuality* (New York: Pantheon)

—— (1979 [1975]), *Discipline and Punish: The Birth of the Prison*, translated by Alan Sheridan (Harmondsworth: Penguin)

—— (1983) Afterword: The Subject and Power. In H. Dreyfus and P. Rainbow (eds) *Michel Foucault: Beyond Structuralism and Hermeneutics*, 2nd edition (Chicago: University of Chicago Press)

Foundation for Information Policy Research (2001) FIPR Release 16/10/2001: Emergency Powers Allow Mass Surveillance for Non-Terrorist Investigations. <uk.eurorights.org/lists/ukcdr-announce/2001-October/000029.html>

Fox, R.G. (1987) Dr Schwitzgebel's Machine Revisited: Electronic Monitoring of Offenders. *Australia and New Zealand Journal of Criminology* Vol. 20

France, M., Kerstetter, J., Black, J., Salkever, A. and Carney, D. (2001) Privacy in an Age of Terror. *Business Week*, November 5 <http://businessweek.com/magazine/content/01_45/b375600/.htm>

Friedman, D. (2000) Privacy and Technology. *Social Philosophy and Policy* Vol. 17 No. 2

Fukuyama, F. (2002) *Our Posthuman Future* (London: Profile Books)

Gall, S.(1994) *News from the Front: A Television Reporter's Life* (London: Heinemann)

Gallagher, D.F. (2001) For The Errant Heart, a Chip that Packs a Wallop. *The New York Times* (Circuits), August 16

Gandy, O. (1993) *The Panoptic Sort: A Political Economy of Personal Information* (Boulder, CO: Westview Press)

—— (1998) Coming to Terms with the Panoptic Sort. In D. Lyon and E. Zureik (eds) *Computers, Surveillance and Privacy* (Minneapolis: Minnesota University Press)

—— (2001) Dividing Practices: Segmentation and Targeting in the Emerging Public Sphere. In W. Bennett and R. Entman (eds) *Mediated Politics: Communication in the Future of Democracy* (Cambridge: Cambridge University Press)

Garfinkel, S. (2000) *Database Nation: The Death of Privacy in the 21st Century* (Sebastopol, CA: O'Reilly and Associates)

Garland, D. (1996) The Limits of State Sovereignty. *British Journal of Criminology* Vol. 36 No. 4

Gates, W. (with Hemingway, C.) (1999) *Business @ the Speed of Thought: Using a Digital Nervous System* (New York: Warner Books)

Geary, J. (2002) *The Body Electric: An Anatomy of the New Bionic Senses* (London: Weidenfield)

George, M. (2002) Intensive Supervision and Surveillance Programmes. *Care and Health Guide* Issue 13, May

Ghandhi, P.R. (2002) *Blackstone's International Human Rights Documents*, 3rd edition (Oxford: Oxford University Press)

Gibbs, A. and King, D. (2002) *The Electronic Ball and Chain? The Development, Operation and Impact of Home Detention in New Zealand* (Dunedin, New Zealand: University of Otago)

Giddens, A. (1985) *The Nation State and Violence* (Cambridge: Polity Press)

—— (1991) *Modernity and Self-Identity: Self and Society in the Late Modern Age* (Cambridge: Polity Press)

—— (1994) *Beyond Left and Right* (Cambridge: Polity Press)

Gilbert, M. (1989) *Second World War* (London: Weidenfeld and Nicolson)

Gill, S. (1995) The Global Panopticon: The Neoliberal State, Economic Life and Democratic Surveillance. *Alternatives* Vol. 20 No. 1

Goffman, E. (1959) *The Presentation of Self in Everyday Life* (Harmondsworth: Penguin)

Goldenberg, S. (2002) Big Brother Will Be Watching America. *Guardian*, November 23

Goodman, M. (1997) Why the Police Don't Care About Computer Crime. *Harvard Journal of Law and Technology* Vol. 10

Gottfredson, G. and Hirschi, T. (1990) *A General Theory of Crime* (Stanford: Stanford University Press)

Government, Internet Industry in Anti-Terror Eavesdropping Partnership (2002) *SiliconValley.com*, May 26 <http://www.siliconvalley.com>

Grabosky, P. and Smith, R. (1998) *Crime in the Digital Age: Controlling Communications and Cyberspace Illegalities* (New Jersey: Transaction Publishers)

—— (2001) Telecommunication Fraud in the Digital Age: The Convergence of Technologies. In D.S. Wall (ed.) *Crime and the Internet* (London: Routledge)

Graham, S. (1998) Spaces of Surveillant Simulation. *Environment and Planning: Society and Space* Vol. 16

Graham, S. and Marvin, S. (2001) *Splintering Urbanism: Networked Infrastructure, Technological Mobilities and the Urban Condition* (London: Routledge)

Greek, C. (2000) The Cutting Edge: A Survey of Technological Innovation. *Federal Probation* Vol. 64 No. 1

Green, H., Himelstein, L., Hof, R.D. and Kunii, I. (1999) The Information Gold Mine. *Business Week*, July 26

Greene, T.C. (2001) Brain-scans Can Defeat Terrorism, InfoSeek Founder Claims. *Register*, October 3. <http://www.theregister.co.uk/content/57/22020.html>

Greening, D. (2000) Data Mining on the Web: There's Gold in that Mountain of Data. *New Architect*, January <www.webtechniques.com/archives/2000/01/greening>

Guardian (2001) Asylum Seekers to be Given ID Cards, October 30 <politics.guardian.co.uk/Whitehall/story/D,,583304,00.html>

Haggerty, K. and Ericson, R.V. (2000) The Surveillant Assemblage. *British Journal of Sociology* Vol. 51 No. 4

Halberstam, D.(1979) *The Powers That Be* (New York: Dell)

Halliday, J. (2001) *Making Punishment Work: Report of a Review of the Sentencing Framework for England and Wales* (London: Home Office)

Hamelink, C. (2000) *The Ethics of Cyberspace* (London: Sage)

Hansard (2002) Computer Misuse Act 1990 Statistics, Hansard, March 26, 1991–2000 <http://www.publications.parliament.uk/pa/ld200102/ldhansrd/vo020125/text/20326w02.htm#20326w02_spmin0>

Harvey, D. (1996) *Justice, Nature and the Geography of Difference* (Oxford: Blackwell)

Hausman, D. and McPherson, M.(1996) *Economic Analysis and Moral Philosophy* (Cambridge: Cambridge University Press)

Havel, V. (1999) Kosovo and the End of the Nation-State. *New York Review of Books*, April 29

Held, D. (1995) Democracy and the New International Order. In D. Archibugi and D. Held (eds) *Cosmopolitan Democracy: An Agenda For a New World Order* (Cambridge: Polity Press)

Held, D., McGrew, A., Goldblatt, D. and Perraton, J. (1999) *Global Transformations* (Cambridge: Polity Press)

Hirst, P. (2001) *War and Power in the 21st Century* (Cambridge: Polity Press)

Home Office (2000) *Criminal Justice and Court Services Act 2000: Explanatory Notes* (London: Home Office)

—— (2002) *Justice for All* (London: Home Office)

Horne, A. (1988) *Macmillan: Volume 1, 1894–1956* (London: Macmillan)

—— (1989) *Macmillan: Volume 2, 1957–1986* (London: Macmillan)

Howard League (1988) *The Community, Punishment and Custody: The Response of the Howard League for Penal Reform to The Green Paper 'Punishment, Custody and the Community'* (London: Howard League)

Huber, P. and Mills, M.P. (2002) How Technology Will Defeat Terrorism. *City Journal* Vol. 12 No. 1 <www.city-journal.org/html/12_1_how_tech.html>

Hughes, T.P. (1983) *Networks of Power* (Baltimore: Johns Hopkins University Press)

Human Development Report (2002) *Deepening Democracy in a Fragmented World*. United Nations Development Programme (UNDP) (New York: Oxford University Press)

Ignatieff, M. (2002) Barbarians at the Gate? *New York Review of Books*, February 28

Information Commissioner (n.d.) Crime and Disorder At 1988: Data Protection Implications for Information Sharing. <dataprotection.gov.uk/dpr/drdoc.nsf/wwwsearch?openform>

Innes, J. (2001) Control Creep. *Sociological Research Online* Vol. 6 No. 3 <http://www.sacresonline.org.uk/6/3/innes.html>

Institute of Criminology (2000) *Future Directions for Community Penalties: Key Conclusions of the 24th Cropwood Conference 28–29 June 2000* (Cambridge: Institute of Criminology)

IScjIS (Integration of Scottish criminal justice Information Systems) (1999) *Bulletin* Edition No. 5, May

Johnston, W. and Grinter, A. (1998) Global Positioning – Don't Call it a Revolution. *Journal of Offender Monitoring*, Spring

Jones, R. (2000) Digital Rule: Punishment, Control and Technology. *Punishment and Society* Vol. 2 No. 1

Kaldor, M. (1999) *New and Old Wars: Organised Violence in a Global Era* (Cambridge: Polity Press)

Kang, J. (1998) Information Privacy in Cyberspace Transactions. *Stanford Law Review* Vol. 50 No. 4

Khong, W.K. (2001) Spam Law for the Internet. *Journal of Information, Law and Technology (JILT)* No. 3 <http://elj.warwick.ac.uk/jilt/01–3/khong.html/> (checked January 1, 2002)

Knightley, P. (2000) *The First Casualty: The War Correspondent as Hero and Myth-maker from the Crimea to Kosovo* (London: Prion Books)

Lacquer, W. (1980) *The Terrible Secret: An Investigation Into the Suppression of Information about Hitler's 'Final Solution'* (London: Weidenfeld and Nicolson)

Lasch, C. (1995) *The Revolt of the Elite and the Betrayal of Democracy* (New York: Norton)

Law Commission (1997) *Legislating the Criminal Code: Misuse of Trade Secrets* (Consultation Paper 150). <http://www.lawcom.gov.uk/library/lccp150/summary.htm>

Lessig, L. (1999) *Code, and Other Laws of Cyberspace* (New York: Basic Books)

Levi, M. (2001) Between the Risk and the Reality Falls the Shadow: Evidence and Urban Legends in Computer Fraud (with apologies to TS Eliot). In D.S. Wall (ed.) *Crime and the Internet* (London: Routledge)

Levi, P. (1979) *If This Is A Man* (Harmondsworth: Penguin)

Lianos, M. and Douglas M. (2000) Dangerization and the End of Deviance: The Institutional Environment. *British Journal of Criminology* Vol. 40 No. 2

Liautaud, B. (2001) Q&A. *PC Magazine*, February 20 <http://www.pcmag.com/print_article/0,3048,a=5368,000.asp>

Lilly, J.R. and Nellis, M. (2001) Home Detention Curfew and the Future of Electronic Monitoring. *Prison Service Journal* Issue 135, May

Lindorff, D. (2002) Grounded <http://www.salon.com/news/feature/2002/11/15/no_fly/index_np.html> (visited December 2002)

Lobley, D. and Smith, D. (2000) *Evaluation of Electronically Monitored Restriction of Liberty Orders* (Edinburgh: Scottish Executive Central Research Unit)

London, L.(2000) *Whitehall and the Jews, 1933–48: British Immigration Policy and the Holocaust* (Cambridge: Cambridge University Press)

Luttwak, E. (1996) A Post-Heroic Military Policy. *Foreign Affairs* Vol. 75 No. 4, July/August

Lyon, D. (1994) *The Electronic Eye: The Rise of Surveillance Society* (Minneapolis: University of Minnesota Press)

—— (2001a) *Surveillance Society: Monitoring Everyday Life* (Buckingham: Open University Press)

—— (2001b) Surveillance after September 11. *Sociological Research Online*, Vol. 6 No. 3 <http://www.socresonline.org.uk/6/3/lyon.html>

—— (2002a) *Surveillance as Social Sorting: Privacy, Risk and Digital Discrimination* (London: Routledge)

—— (2002b) Surveillance Studies: Understanding Visibility, Mobility and the Phenetic Fix. *Surveillance and Society* Vol. 1 No. 1 <http://www.surveillance-and-society.org>

Madsen, W. (2001) Homeland Security, Homeland Profits. CorpWatch, December 21 <http://www.corpwatch.org/issues/PID.jsp?articleid=1108>

Mair, G. (2001) Technology and the Future of Community Penalties. In A.E. Bottoms, L. Gelsthorpe and S. Rex (eds) *Community Penalties: Change and Challenges* (Cullompton, Devon: Willan)

Mandeles, M.D., Hone, T.C. Terry and S.S. (1996) *Managing 'Command and Control' in the Persian Gulf War* (Westport, CT: Praeger)

Maney, K. (2001) What Can Tech Companies Do? *USA Today*, September 19

Marx, G.T. (1988) *Undercover: Police Surveillance in America* (Berkeley, CA: University of California Press)

—— (1995) The Engineering of Social Control: The Search for the Silver Bullet. In J. Hagan and R. Peterson (eds) *Crime and Inequality* (Stanford, CA: Stanford University Press)

—— (2002) What's New About the 'New Surveillance'? Classifying Change and Continuity. *Surveillance and Society* Vol. 1 No. 1 <http://www.surveillance-and-society.org>

—— (forthcoming) *Windows Into the Soul: Surveillance Society in an Age of High Technology* (Chicago: University of Chicago Press)

Mathieson, T. (1997) The Viewer Society: Foucault's Panopticon Revisited. *Theoretical Criminology* Vol. 1 No. 2

McNeil, F. (2001) Dancing to Different Tunes? A Scottish Commentary on a 'New Choreography'. *Vista: Perspectives on Probation* Vol. 7 No. 1

Meek, J. (2002) Towns Secretly Testing 'Spy' Software. *Guardian*, June 13

Melossi, D. (1994) Normal Crimes, Elites and Social Control. In D. Nelken (ed.) *The Futures of Criminology* (London: Sage)

Mitnick, K. (2002) *The Art of Deception: Controlling the Human Element of Security* (New York: John Wiley and Sons)

Monmonier, M. (2002), *Spying with Maps: Surveillance Technologies and the Future of Privacy* (Chicago: University of Chicago Press)

Moore, A. (2000) Privacy and the Encryption Debate. *Knowledge, Technology and Policy* Vol. 12 No. 4, Winter

Morrison, D. and Tumber, H. (1988) *Journalists at War: The Dynamics of News-reporting During the Falklands* (London: Constable)

Morton, O.(1995) Defence Technology: The Information Advantage. *Economist*, June 10

Mowlana, H., Gerbner, G. and Schiller, H.I. (eds) (1992) *Triumph of the Image: The Media's War in the Persian Gulf: A Global Perspective* (Boulder, CO: Westview Press)

Murray, Frank J. (2002) NASA Plans to Read Terrorist's Minds at Airports. *Washington Times*, August 17 <http://www.washtimes.com/national/20020817-704732.htm> (visited December 2002)

Nash, M. (1999) Enter the Polibation Officer. *International Journal of Police Science and Management* Vol. 1 No. 4

National Strategy for Homeland Security (2002, July) US Office of Homeland Security. <http://www.whitehouse.gov/homeland/book/nat_strat_hls.pdf>

NCIS (1998) Europol, the First Ever EU Criminal Intelligence Agency Goes Live. Press Release 16/98 September 30 <ncis.co.ukncis/web/Press%20Releases/EUROPOL>

NCIS (1999a) Project Trawler: Crime on the Information Highways. <ncis.co.uk/ncis/newpage1.htm>

NCIS (1999b) Police Support Home Secretary's Announcement on Schengen Participation. Press Release 07/99 March 12. <ncis.co.ukncis/web/Press%20Releases/SCHENGEN>

Nef, J.U. (1950) *War and Human Progress* (Cambridge, MA: Harvard University Press)

Nellis, M. (1989) Keeping Tags on the Underclass. *Social Work Today*, May 25

—— (1991) The Electronic Monitoring of Offenders in England and Wales: Recent Developments and Future Prospects. *British Journal of Criminology* Vol. 31 No. 2

—— (1993) Electronic Monitoring: Grounds for Resistance? In J.R. Lilly and J. Himan (eds) *The Electronic Monitoring of Offenders: Second Series* (Leicester: De Montfort University Law Monographs)

—— (2000) Law and Order: The Electronic Monitoring of Offenders. In D. Dolowitz, with R. Hulme, M. Nellis and F. O'Neill (eds) *Policy Transfer and British Social Policy* (Milton Keynes: Open University Press)

—— (2001) Interview with Tom Stacey. *Prison Service Journal* Issue 135, May

—— (2003) News Media, Popular Culture and the Electronic Monitoring of Offenders in England and Wales. *Howard Journal of Criminal Justice* Vol. 42 No. 1

Nellis, M. and Lilly, J.R. (2000) Accepting the Tag: Probation and Home Detention Curfew. *Vista: Perspectives on Probation* Vol. 6 No. 1

New York Times (2001a) September 18 <nytimes.com/2001/09/18/national/18RULE.htm> Registration required

New York Times (2001b) October 1 <http://www.nytimes.com/2001/10/01/international/europe/01GERM.html> Registration required

Norris, C. (2002) From Personal to Digital: CCTV, the Panopticon and the Technological Mediation of Suspicion and Social Control. In D. Lyon (ed.) *Surveillance as Social Sorting: Privacy, Risk and Digital Discrimination* (London: Routledge)

Norris, C. and G. Armstrong (1999) *The Maximum Surveillance Society: The Rise of CCTV* (Oxford: Berg)

O'Harrow, Jr., Robert (2002) Intricate Screening of Fliers in Works. *Washington Post*, January 31 <http://www.washingtonpost.com/wp-dyn/articles/A5185-2002Jan31.html> (visited December 2002)

Oettinger, A.G. (1990) *Whence and Whither Intelligence, Command and Control? The Certainty of Uncertainty* (Cambridge, MA: Program on Information Resources Policy, Harvard University)

Ofori, K. (1999) *When Being No. 1 is Not Enough: The Impact of Advertising Practices on Minority Owned & Minority Formatted Broadcast Stations.* Report to the Federal Communications Commission. Civil Rights Forum on Communications Policy, Washington DC

Pease, K. (2001) *Crime Futures and Foresight: Challenging Criminal Behaviour in the Information Age.* In D.S. Wall (ed.) *Crime and the Internet* (London: Routledge)

Peppers, D. and Rogers, M. (1997) *The 1:1 Future: Building Relationships One Customer at a Time* (Norfolk: Currency)

Peters, A. (1986) Main Currents in Criminal Law Theory. In J. van Dike et al. (eds) *Criminal Law in Action* (Arnhem: Gouda Quint)

Phillips, D. and Curry, M. (2002) Privacy and the Phenetic Urge: Geodemographics and the Changing Spatiality of Local Practice. In D. Lyon (ed.) *Surveillance as Social Sorting: Privacy, Risk and Digital Discrimination* (London: Routledge)

Pitts, J. (2000) The New Correctionalism: Young People, Youth Justice and New Labour. In R. Matthews and J. Pitts (eds) *Crime, Disorder and Community Safety* (London: Routledge)

Ponting, C. (1999) *The Pimlico History of the Twentieth Century* (London: Pimlico Press) Previously published 1998, as *Progress and Barbarism: The World in the Twentieth Century* (London: Chatto and Windus)

Poster, M. (1995) *The Second Media Age* (Cambridge: Polity Press)

Power, S.(2002) *A Problem from Hell: America and the Age of Genocide* (New York: Basic Books)

Predictive Networks (2001) *Digital Silhouettes* <predictivenetworks.com>

Preston, P. (2001) *Reshaping Communications* (London: Sage)

Prison Privatisation Report International (2002) Bulletin No. 47 (London: University of Greenwich Pubic Services International Research Unit) <psiru.org/justice>

R v. *Fellows and R* v. *Arnold* (1996) (Court of Appeal, Criminal Division). *The Times*, October 3

Raab, C. (1997) Co-Producing Data Protection: *International Review of Law Computers and Technology*, Vol. 11

—— (1998) Electronic Confidence: Trust, Information and Public Administration. In I. Snellen and W. van de Donk (eds) *Public Administration in an Information Age: A Handbook* (Amsterdam: IOS Press)

—— (2001) Electronic Service Delivery in the UK: Proaction and Privacy Protection. In J. Prins (ed.) *Designing E-Government: On the Crossroads of Technological Innovation and Institutional Change* (Boston and The Hague: Kluwer Law International)

Raab, C. and Bennett, C. (1996) Taking the Measure of Privacy: Can Data Protection Be Evaluated? *International Review of Administrative Sciences* Vol. 62

Read, G. (1990) Electronic Monitoring is a Costly Distraction. *The Magistrate*, Vol. 46 No. 8

Reidenberg, J. (1997) Governing Networks and Rule-Making in Cyberspace. In B. Kahin and C. Nesson (eds) *Borders in Cyberspace: Information Policy and the Global Information Infrastructure* (Cambridge, MA: MIT Press)

Reiner, R. (2000) *The Politics of the Police*, 3rd edition (Oxford: Oxford University Press)

Renzema, M. (1998a) GPS: Is Now the Time to Adopt? *Journal of Offender Monitoring*, Spring

—— (1998b) Satellite Monitoring of Offenders: A Report from the Field. *Journal of Offender Monitoring*, Spring

—— (1999) GPS Users Report Positive Experiences. *Journal of Offender Monitoring*, Summer

—— (2000) Tracking GPS: A Third Look. *Journal of Offender Monitoring*, Spring

Rheingold, H. (1993) *The Virtual Community: Homesteading on the Electronic Frontier* (Reading, MA: Addison Wesley)

Riley, D. and Shaw, M. (1985) *Parental Supervision and Juvenile Delinquency. Home Office Research Study 83* (London: Home Office)

Robertson, G. (1999) *Crimes Against Humanity: The Struggle for Global Justice* (Harmondsworth: Penguin)

Roberts-Witt, S. (2001), Gold diggers. *PC Magazine*, February 20 <http://www.pcmag.com/print_article/0,3048,a=5368,000.asp>

Rose, N. (2000) The Biology of Culpability: Pathological Identity and Crime Control in a Biological Culture. *Theoretical Criminology* Vol. 4 No. 1

Rosen, J. (2000) *The Unwanted Gaze: The Destruction of Privacy in America* (New York: Vintage)

Rothleder, N., Harris, E. and Bloedorn, E. (n.d.) *Focusing on the Data in Data Mining: Lessons from Recent Experience. Online report* The MITRE Corporation <http://www.mitre.org>

Rule, J. (1998) High-tech Workplace Surveillance: What's Really New? In D. Lyon and E. Zureik (eds) *Computers, Surveillance and Privacy* (Minneapolis: Minnesota University Press)

Scheerer, S. (2000) Three Trends into the New Millennium: The Managerial, the Populist and the Trend towards Global Justice. In P. Green and A. Rutherford (eds) *Criminal Justice in Transition* (Oxford: Hart Publishing)

Scheeres, J. (2002) Europe Passes Snoop Measure. *WIRED News*, May 30 <http://www.wired.com/news/print/0,1294,52882,00.html>

Schiller, H.I. (1981) *Who Knows: Information in the Age of the Fortune 500* (Norwood, NJ: Ablex)

—— (2000) *Living in the Number One Country: Reflections from a Critic of American Empire* (New York: Seven Stories Press)

Scottish Executive (2000) *The Electronic Monitoring of Offenders: Consultation Document* (Edinburgh: Scottish Executive)

—— (2001) *The Electronic Monitoring of Offenders: Results of Consultation* (Edinburgh: Scottish Executive)

Secretary of State for Defence (1996) *Statement of the Defence Estimates* Cm 3223, May

Sennett, R. (1978) *The Fall of Public Man: On the Social Psychology of Capitalism* (New York: Vintage)

Shaw, M. (1991) *Post-Military Society: Militarism, Demilitarization and War at the End of the Twentieth Century* (Cambridge: Polity Press)

Smith, D. (2001) Electronic Monitoring of Offenders: The Scottish Experience. *Criminal Justice* Vol. 1 No. 2

Smith, G. (1998) Electronic Pearl Harbor? Not Likely. *Issues in Science and Technology* Vol. 15, Fall. <http://www.nap.edu/issues/15.1/smith.htm>

Smith, H. (ed.) (1992) *The Media and the Gulf War: The Press and Democracy in Wartime* (Washington: Seven Locks Press)

Sovern, J. (1999) Opting In, Opting Out, or No Options At All: The Fight for Control of Personal Information. *Washington Law Review* Vol. 74 No. 4

Sparks, R. (2000a) Perspectives on Risk and Penal Politics. In T. Hope and R. Sparks (eds) *Crime, Risk and Insecurity* (London: Routledge)

—— (2000b) Risk and Blame in Criminal Justice Controversies: British Press Coverage and Official Discourse on Prison Security 1993–6. In J. Pratt and M. Brown (eds) *Dangerous Offenders: Punishment and Social Order* (London: Routledge)

Speer, D. (2000) Redefining Borders: The Challenges of Cybercrime. *Crime, Law and Social Change* Vol. 34 No. 3

St Jorre, J. (1983), The Infotech Dream: IRIS. *Observer*, April 17 and 24

Stanley, J. and Steinhardt, B. (2002) Drawing a Blank: The Failure of Facial Recognition in Tampa, Florida. An ACLU Special Report. Washington DC: American Civil Liberties Union. <http://archive.aclu.org/issues/privacy/drawing_blank.pdf> (accessed May 7, 2003)

Stacey, T. (1989) Why Tagging Should be Used to Reduce Incarceration. *Social Work Today*, April 20

—— (1993) Toward the Tracking Tag. In J.R. Lilly and J. Himan (eds) *The Electronic Monitoring of Offenders: Second Series* (Leicester: De Montfort University Law Monographs)

—— (1995a) Special Applications of Electronic Monitoring. In K. Schulz (ed.) *Electronic Monitoring and Corrections: The Policy, the Operation, the Research* (Vancouver: Simon Fraser University)

—— (1995b) Innovations in Technology. In K. Schulz (ed.) *Electronic Monitoring and Corrections: The Policy, the Operation, the Research* (Vancouver: Simon Fraser University)

Steinberg, J. (2001) In Sweeping Campus Canvasses, US Checks on MidEast Students. *New York Times,* November 12 <nytimes.com/2001/11/12/nationa/12STUD.html>

Stepanek, M. (2000) Weblining. *Business Week,* April 3

Streitfeld, D. and Piller, C. (2002) Big Brother Finds All in Once-wary High Tech *LATimes.com,* January 19 <http://www.latimes.com/news/nation-world/nation/la-011902techshift.story>

Sullivan, B. (2001) Warming to Big Brother. *MSNBC.com,* November 14 <http://www.msnbc.com/news/654959.asp?cp1=1>

Sunstein, C. (2001) *Republic.com* (New Haven: Princeton University Press)

Taylor, F.W. (1964), *Scientific Management* (London: Harper and Row)

Taylor, P.M. (1992) *War and the Media: Propaganda and Persuasion in the Gulf War* (Manchester: Manchester University Press)

Taylor, P. (2001) Hacktivism: In Search of Lost Ethics? In D.S. Wall (ed.) *Crime and the Internet* (London: Routledge)

Thomas, D. and Loader, B. (eds) (2000) *Cybercrime: Law Enforcement, Security and Surveillance in the Information Age* (New York and London: Routledge)

Thompson, E.P. (1980) *Writing by Candlelight* (London: Merlin)

Thrift, N. and French S. (2002) The Automatic Production of Space. *Transactions of the Institute of British Geographers* Vol. 27 No. 4

Tildesley, W.M. and Bullock, W.F. (1983) Curfew Orders: The Arguments For. *Probation Journal,* Vol. 30 No. 4

Toffler, A. and Toffler, H. (1993) *War and Anti-War* (Boston: Little, Brown)

Tomlinson, J. (1999) *Globalization and Culture* (Cambridge: Polity Press)

Toronto Star (2001) New ID Cards for Landed Immigrants, October 11

Tumber, H. (2002) Reporting Under Fire. Paper at conference on Communicating Conflict – War and the Media (New York University/Goldsmiths College: London, May 10)

Tunick, M. (2000) Privacy in the Face of New Technologies of Surveillance. *Public Affairs Quarterly* Vol. 14 No. 3

Tyska, L.A. and Fennelly, L.J. (1998) *150 Things You Should Know About Security* (Oxford: Butterworth-Heinemann)

Underwood, S. (1997) *Securicor: The People Business* (Oxford: CPL Books)

United Kingdom (UK), Cm 3438 (1996) *Government.Direct* (London: The Stationery Office)

United Kingdom (UK), Home Office (1998) *Crime and Disorder Partnerships: Disclosure of Information in Connection with Crime and Disorder – Joint Statement by the Home Office and Data Protection Registrar.* <homeoffice.gov.uk/cdact/jsdprho.htm>

United Kingdom (UK), Cm 4310 (1999) *Modernising Government* (London: The Stationery Office)

United Kingdom (UK), Home Office (1999) *The Crime and Disorder Act: Guidance on Statutory Crime and Disorder Partnerships.* <homeoffice.gov.uk/cdact/atcgch5.htm>

United Kingdom (UK), Office of the E-Envoy (2001) *E-Government Metadata Framework* (London: Office of the E-Envoy)

United Kingdom (UK), Cm 5557 (2002) *Entitlement Cards and Identity Fraud* (London: The Stationery Office)

United Kingdom (UK), House of Commons (2002) *Information Commissioner – Annual Report and Accounts for the Year Ending 31 March 2002* HC 913,

June (London: The Stationery Office)

United Kingdom (UK), Performance and Innovation Unit, Cabinet Office (2002) *Privacy and Data-Sharing* (London: The Stationery Office)

United States Foreign Intelligence Surveillance Court (2002) *Memorandum Opinion*, May 17

United States of America v. Robert A. Thomas and Carleen Thomas (1996) 74 *F.3d* 701; 1996 *U.S. App. Lexis* 1069; 1996 *Fed App.* 0032P (6th Cir.)

Urry, J. (1999) Mediating Global Citizenship. *iichiko intercultural* Vol. 11

—— (2000) *Sociology Beyond Societies: Mobilities for the Twenty-First Century* (London: Routledge)

USA PATRIOT Act of 2001, Pub. L. No. 107–56, 115 Stat. 272 (2001)

Van Vogt, A.E. (1963) *The Great Judge: In, Away and Beyond* (London: Panther)

Veale, S. (2001) Word for Word/Pentagon Science Fair; Wanted: Tools to Fight Terrorism. All Suggestions Welcome. *New York Times*, October 28 Section 4

Victorian, A. (1999) *Mind Controllers* (London: Satin Publications)

Walker, C. (2002) *Blackstone's Guide to the Anti-Terrorism Legislation* (Oxford: Oxford University Press)

Wall, D.S. (1997) Policing the Virtual Community: The Internet, Cyber-crimes and the Policing of Cyberspace . In P. Francis, P. Davies and V. Jupp (eds) *Policing Futures* (London: Macmillan)

—— (1999) Cybercrimes: New Wine, No Bottles? In P. Davies, P. Francis and V. Jupp (eds) *Invisible Crimes: Their Victims and Their Regulation* (London: Macmillan)

—— (2000) The Theft of Electronic Services: Telecommunications and Tele-services. Essay 1 on the CD-ROM annex to DTI *Turning the Corner* (London: Department of Trade and Industry)

—— (2001) Maintaining Order and Law on the Internet. In D.S. Wall (ed.) *Crime and the Internet* (London: Routledge)

—— (2002a) Insecurity and the Policing of Cyberspace. In A. Crawford (ed.) *Crime and Insecurity* (Cullompton, Devon: Willan)

—— (2002b) Spams and Scams, the 'White Noise of Cyberspace': The Problem of Small Impact Multiple Victimisation Deceptions on the Internet. Paper at American Society of Criminology Annual Conference, Chicago, November

—— (2002c) DOT.CONS: Internet Related Frauds and Deceptions upon Individuals within the UK, Final Report to the Home Office, March (unpublished)

Walter, I., Sugg, D. and Moore, L. (2001) *A Year on the Tag: Interviews with Criminal Justice and Electronic Monitoring Staff about Curfew Orders. Home Office Research Findings 140* (London: Home Office)

Walters, J. (2002) Why Only Satellites Can Stop Gridlock. *Observer*, February 24

Wasserstein, B. (1988 [1979]) *Britain and the Jews of Europe, 1939–1945* (Oxford: Oxford University Press)

Webster, F. (1995) *Theories of the Information Society* (London: Routledge)

—— (2001) Information Warfare: Changing Forms and Changing Reasons for War. In Mark Ulam (ed.) *Reconstructuring the Means of Violence: Defence Restructuring and Conversion.* COST Action A10 (Luxemburg: European Commission)

Webster, F. and Robins, K. (1986) *Information Technology: A Luddite Analysis* (Norwood, NJ: Ablex)

Wells, H.G. (1938) *World Brain* (London: Methuen)

Westin, A.F. (1967) *Privacy and Freedom* (New York: Atheneum)

Whitaker, R. (1999) *The End of Privacy: How Total Surveillance is Becoming a Reality* (New York: The New Press)

Whitfield, D. (1997) *Tackling the Tag: The Electronic Monitoring of Offenders* (Winchester: Waterside Press)

—— (2001) *The Magic Bracelet: Technology and Offender Supervision* (Winchester: Waterside Press)

Windelsham, D. (2001) *Dispensing Justice: Responses to Crime volume 4* (Oxford: Oxford University Press)

Wright, S. (1998) *An Appraisal of the Technologies of Political Control: Interim STOA Report (PE 166.499)* (Luxembourg: European Parliament, Directorate General for Research, Directorate A, The STOA Programme)

Yaukey, J. (2001) Common Sense Can Help You Cope with Spam. *USA Today*, December 19 <http://www.usatoday.com/life/cyber/ccarch/2001/12/19/yaukey.htm>

Zonderman, J. (1990) *Beyond The Crime Lab: The New Science of Investigation* (New York: Wiley and Sons)

Index

Compiled by Sue Carlton